Menarche

Cover design and layout Rachael Hertogs

Cover Photo; Ruby and the Red Tent taken by © Brigid Brightfire, featuring Ruby Sanger

Quotes used in this booklet are used by kind permission of the authors:
page 35 © Alexandra Pope

pages 37, 38, 39, 41 Reprinted from *Women's Bodies, Women's Wisdom* © 2010, Christiane Northrup, M.D

pages 38, 39 © Brooke Medicine Eagle

page 39 Reprinted from *The Red Tent* © Anita Diamant, 1997

Diagrams, photos and art work must not be reproduced without permission.

We welcome articles, stories, pictures from all women; this booklet is updated regularly and we would love new articles to add to it.
email: info@rachaelhertogs.co.uk
Join the web group https://www.facebook.com/pages/Moon-Lodge

Please Note- We are not Medical Doctors. This information is for educational purposes only and is not intended to be used as substitute for medical advice or used to diagnose any disease. Please use good judgment when reading all materials.

First produced May 04, this issue updated February 2013

ISBN-13: 978-1492135982
ISBN-10: 1492135984

Praise for Menarche- A Journey into Womanhood

"A practical, supportive and very informative book which shares women's wisdom with girls embarking on their first periods in an accessible way. I love the way you have left space on its pages for them to add their own wisdom. That is really special."

Lucy H Pearce contributing editor at JUNO magazine and author of Moon Time: a guide to celebrating your menstrual cycle and Moods of Motherhood www.happywomb.com

"I bought this book as gift for my daughter and for the beloved daughter of one of my best friends. Cannot rate it enough - just a wonderful positive statement for teen women."
Linda, Sussex

"Rachael's Menarche book is a veritable feast supporting any young woman on her menstrual journey. It is easy to read, full of stories and experiences from women of all ages and cultures, and a very welcome and beautiful tool which may inspire the maiden woman to celebrate her movement into womanhood. In a culture often lacking in knowing how to support teenage transitions, we must receive gifts such as this book with open arms and open heart. It offers practical self care of the menstrual cycle, tools for supporting the emotional aspects of a cycle with self-enquiry exercises, and a rich and diverse offering of lore of menstruation around the world, experiences, wonderings, quotes and wisdom.
Any menstruating woman who didn't feel she received the menarche celebration she wanted, or the wisdom she needed to bring health to her cycle, would benefit form reading this book as well as all young girls approaching menarche. Rachael has long held a place for transforming experience and perceptions around menstruation. Thank you Rachael. "

Dominique Sakoilsky author of Seven Secrets of a Joyful Birth, founder of Relaxed Birth and Parenting, Active Birth Teacher, counsellor and cranio sacral therapist, Bristol. www.relaxedbirthandparenting.com

"For any mother or mother and daughter wanting to welcome her daughter's menstruation in a loving and positive way this book is a wonderful tool of focus. A lovely blend of creative ideas and practical knowledge, also the reader is encouraged to explore within themselves as to what feels comfortable for them. Rachael is very open about her experience of listening to her daughters wishes at the time of her first bleed and letting go her own desires of how best to welcome menarche. This is an inspiring book, a book that encourages us to question and discover for ourselves. I will be very happy to recommend this book to clients and students."

Amanda Rayment. Master herbalist and Practitioner.
www.welcomeworldcafe.com

"What a wonderful resource this is for young woman entering menarche. I wish that I had had access to such wise insightful information when I started my own menarche. Rachael weaves her insights and tips in a easy to read joyful way and offers young and older woman alike a refreshing new reference point on which to view this female journey. I will be sharing it with my nieces and granddaughter without a doubt. Thank you for sharing your wisdom Rachael ."

Louise Bennett, founder of Relaxed Birth and Parenting
www.relaxedbirthandparenting.com

Menarche
a journey into womanhood

a mums and girls guide to celebrating her first period!

By Rachael Hertogs

For Tabitha, my first born, who inspired me to make the world a better place

Contents

Welcome!

Starting your period is a natural process but at first it can be a little scary. You may know what your period is, but still be a little unsure about things when it starts. I remember feeling worried how my friends would feel about me because I thought I was the only one who had started her period.

I was embarrassed to talk to my mum, my sister and my friends about periods. I found it useful to write my feelings in my diary. Now that I am a mum with 2 daughters, my goal has been to make their stages of growing up special. That's why I started helping other mums with Menarche Celebrations and making Menarche booklets and gift sets.

Imagine living in a world that honoured women's bleeding as sacred and special.
There used to be a time, over 30,000 years ago, when it was! These ancient people understood that a woman's bleeding time was a sacred time, a time of deep introspection, a time for her to let go of her responsibilities, to go to the moon lodge, where women would share their wisdom with each other, they would fast (eat special foods), connect to their body-wisdom(listen quietly to their bodies), and they would meditate, sleep and dream.

For most western women of today's modern society just to consider honouring our menstrual blood might seem shocking.

How different would we feel about our bodies and our bleeding if we had been given positive messages of love, beauty, and acceptance?
If society's messages were of support, honouring and approval?
Would we still hide our bleeding-time in shame & ignore our bodies' signals to take time out?
It is time for all women to stop judging each other, to stop judging ourselves and to reconnect as the sisters we are.

Embrace your Menarche and be proud to be a young woman.
This new experience is a significant aspect of your life and it is important that you also express your thoughts and feelings with other women.

Remember, this new change in your life will visit you on a monthly basis for a very long time and the women around you want to make sure you approach this change in the safest and healthiest way possible.

This book is a chance to explore your feelings, thoughts, creativity that comes from being a bleeding woman. May you walk in beauty, *Blessings and love,*
Rachael xxx

I hope that you will share this book with your mum, and any sisters, aunties, friends, cousins, who might be interested.

So where do we start in all of this talk about becoming a woman?
I suggest you begin by asking your mum about her first period!
If you don't have a mum, or can't face asking her...who else could you ask? Maybe a grandmother, an aunty, a family friend, maybe one of your friends mums or older sisters?
You could even get some of your friends together , with their mums and ask them to share their stories with you all.

Here's some first period stories from some of my friends!

"Whenever I have my period, I have the feeling that in spite of all the pain, discomfort and mess, I'm carrying around a sweet secret. So even though it's a nuisance, in a certain way I'm always looking forward to the time when I'll feel that secret inside me once again." Anne Frank

I always had a deep respect for my 'woman's body' – I don't know where it stemmed from– certainly not my mother or sister, but I just knew there was something magical about it!! I must have had a sense it was connected to my cycle as I couldn't wait to start my period– from about 9 years old I was desperate to get it!

Image Rachael with girls group

When it came, at 11, I was surprised at these brown blobs in my knickers (I was expecting bright red blood), and my mother was confused that I was so happy– she said 'that's it now, you have to deal with that every month for years and years.' She gave me a huge fat kotex pad. I had no rites of passage, no guidance, it was hidden away– not celebrated– it was shamed, called 'the curse'. I was confused by how periods related to getting pregnant – even though we had been taught sex education in school- I just couldn't get the connection from the eggs to the blood- how did they work together? I don't recall any mention of the feelings that come with the hormone fluctuations, or any talk of emotions, just facts, and mention of moodiness with PMT and using pain killers to get through the cramps.   I was one of the first in my class to get it- other girls said you could tell when someone was on their period because of the smell- I was so worried I smelled- but *I couldn't* smell anything! I confided in the other girl in my class who had started too- we were both tall, with bigger breasts than the others, we had nothing else in common, but our periods bonded us.

I was sad that no one gave me any positive affirmation about this stage of my becoming a woman- inside I was excited and felt grown up, but no one else recognised that. I carried a loss about that into my late teens and early 20's-and I tried to ease that loss by having relationships with older guys, bad boys who made me feel like I was a woman- when really I was still a girl. Luckily, when I was in my 20's a group of women welcomed me and honoured me as a woman, sang to me, blessed me with oils, and finally supported me in recognising the wild woman I was! **Rachael, West Wales**

My first period; Oh they had told us about it in biology, shown us the things you put in your pants, told us how it happens, and that one day we would have it. But they didn't tell us how it would feel, how it would change our lives, how it would open up a wonderful new chapter.

I started my period on the 12th January 1985, I remember it because of a song on Top of the Pops the same day! It was during a PE lesson at school, I felt a drip, I thought I was wetting myself, but when in the changing rooms afterwards, I took of my PE pants (that we had to wear over our normal knickers because of our silly short PE skirt) and there it was red and dark, a patch of period!

Well luckily it was last lesson, so I hurried home and told my sister, who gave me a pad. I told her not to tell Mom, it was my secret to be revealed by me! I remember my Mom was in bed in her darkened bedroom with a migraine, she had lots of them in those days. I went in to see her, and of course my sister had told her (never could keep a secret) I was a bit embarrassed, but my mom was there, with her hurty head, smiling, and said "congratulations you're a woman now"

What? Me a woman? No, surely not I was but 12 and a half, I had very small breasts and a bizarre triangle of pubic hair, and now I was bleeding, but that didn't make me a woman did it?

I wanted it to stop, I wanted to climb trees, and play outside and not be a woman, I was a child.   **Image: Suzanne and her eldest daughter Abi**

Then after a few days it stopped, and I was a child again. But things were changing. Every month, this magical flow, every month a box of "Vespre" sanitary towels would slowly empty. I was fascinated by it, but no one seemed to want to talk about it, I looked at the women in my life, and the women in the world around me, thinking to myself, they all have this, yet how come we don't know? why was it sooooo secret and hidden? Why did people brush it aside and not talk about it? The girls at school talked about periods, but they mumbled the word, not wanting to speak it loudly. I went to an all girls' school, and remember seeing on many occasions, girls on the "sick bench" curled up in pain, waiting for their parents to pick them up and take them home.

I was very lucky it seemed, yes I got period pain, but it was never curling up bad, all the books described mood swings, and pain, yes I got the mood swings, but not the pain as I had imagined, but still no one will talk about it.

Today there are books that do talk about it, that say that it's not all bad, it's part of BECOMING a woman.

I am now a mother, with 3 daughters of my own, and a step daughter who has recently started her journey to Womanhood, with her Menstruation, that really is a fabulous word, sounds much better than "Period" - more powerful to say "I'm Menstruating!" than "it's THAT time of the month" my advice to my daughters is celebrate it, each is a stage of womanhood, you will only go through it once in your life, it is magical and wonderful. **Suzanne Thomas, Ludlow, UK**

My story is not anything outstanding, but I want to share it anyway. I was born in 1964, when things like that weren't spoken of. I remember my girlfriend, Heather, got her period, and I was waiting for mine, never seemed to show. I was 13 when I finally got mine. I remember feeling uncomfortable that day at school, and was sitting out on the stage after gym class when I noticed blood between my legs. I was so embarrassed. I went to the washroom and cleaned up, and couldn't wait to get home. I got home, changed my clothes and looked in my mother's bathroom for a pad, then put it in place. I gathered courage and seeked her out, then she showed me how to use the elastic belt to hold the pad in place as we had never discussed it before. What a contraption! I remember thinking "this is it?"... a letdown. I saw her whispering on the street to our neighbour about how I got my period, but that was it. As I grew older and had children of my own, I always wanted to have a daughter (didn't happen, but I was blessed with three wonderful boys) so that I could take her out and CELEBRATE her first period – just me and her. Celebrate her next phase in life – becoming a WOMAN, physically feeling a part of the cycle of our Mother Earth. I don't believe it is something to be ashamed of, but something wonderful, signifying growth and change and new awareness. Six years ago I had a hysterectomy, so I no longer shed blood monthly. However, my body still recognizes the changes in each moon cycle, and I am grateful for that. **Debbie Bryer Smiths Falls, Ontario, Canada**

The first time I found out about periods was at school. Just before leaving junior school each girl child was issued with a little pocket sized booklet entitled Personally Yours. I still remember the cover, a fuzzy anonymous image of a reclining girl with a blonde bob, pink jumper and jeans. We were intrigued. We took them outside at lunch break and three of us girl friends, lay on our backs, legs up to the ceiling in a concrete crawling tunnel in the playing field and devoured this new information. We were fascinated, not disgusted in any way. I remember thinking many years later that it was cunning marketing. The booklets were compiled by Tampax. Of course they reassured us that we could still swim or ride a horse. Just use a tampon. I was reassured. It felt exciting, but calm.

For me it was to be three years before I experienced it for myself. I remember being in my flute lesson and bawling my eyes out. I felt muddle-headed, clumsy, frustrated, and very vulnerable. I cried and cried. My poor, male teacher, was as kind and understanding as he could be, I was obviously just having a "bad" day. I went to the toilet after the lesson. And there, to my astonishment, copious birthing red blood on the toilet paper. I felt excited– a sense of knowing that this,this was a big deal for me, for my life. A shift, a change had happened. School was over for the day. But it was a boarding school so I would not be seeing any of my family until the weekend. It felt momentous. I needed to share that I was changed. I grabbed my best friend, and again we went outside. We walked in the gardens and I told her. It felt so right to share it with a female friend.

But being in boarding school also had its downsides. I felt a deep shame. I didn't want anyone else to know that I had my period. So I set up elaborate coughing routines when I opened the crinkly sanitary towel wrapper. I spent ages scouring knickers from leaks, and eventually settled on black pants all the time.

Only trusted friends knew when you were on. We used to watch each other's backs, literally. In the summer term we wore white and blue striped skirts which showed leaks very easily. It was a sisterhood. You knew you were true, trusted

friends if your friend told you she was on. We had a special code word. P. Which then, for reasons unknown to me, became Mr P. Then because my father was Mr P, we called the period Stephen, after my dad. What irony to have a male period. We didn't see that at the time!

Image: Aisling, Lucy Pearce, Merrily & Francesca (my mother)

My mother cried when I told her. And I told my step mother too. They were both lovely and so good with any practical questions I had, there was no awkwardness. But I swore my step mother to secrecy – she was, after all, the sisterhood. But at some point, my father figured out I was menstruating, and was angry and hurt that I had not told him. I got a five page letter of anger. What business is my blood of yours? I wondered. I felt vulnerable for having my privacy, my secrecy, broken, and by a man.

And so it continues to this day. For me my trusted sisterhood knows about my cycles – it gives them insight into "where I'm at", but I find it more difficult to tell my husband and children. It feels like a sacred secret, which I don't trust them so much with, because to them it is something external, which can be judged, or joked about or used against me. For my sisters, they know, they understand, they truly get it, because they've got it too! **Lucy Pearce, Co Cork, Ireland**

I remember vividly the day of my first period. I was educated in a convent in Yorkshire and was in the middle of a maths class when I suddenly realised I had 'started'. I had to wait till the bell went before I could hurry up to the infirmary to ask Sister Cyprian, the school nurse, what I should do. She gave me a paracetamol and sent me down to the 'laundry' to see Sister Sylvester; the nun who looked after our clothing and linen.

I was issued with a strange elastic belt that had clips at the front and back, and a bag full of **enormous** thick white 'Dr White's' sanitary pads. They had loops at each end to attach them to the two clips on the belt, and were disposable.

There was nothing discreet about them! Sister Sylvester told me that this marked the beginning of womanhood – which meant I was now 'unclean' – and sent me on my way telling me that, on no account, must I discuss this with any of my friends who had not already started their periods.

That was nearly forty years ago and I'm SO glad that things have changed! We live in a society now where most of these kinds of taboos, and archaic religious views about our being 'unclean' during, or because of, our moon cycles, have been broken. And we have so much choice when it comes to deciding how to manage our bleeding too! **Brigit Strawbridge, UK**

I got my first period when I was 11 and a half, the summer before starting secondary school. My parents and my older sister and I went to a friend's house for a summer garden bbq party with quite a few people. During the evening I went to the toilet and discovered blood in my knickers

I wasn't expecting it so didn't have any sanitary pads or anything with me, so had to use lots of toilet paper in my knickers. I kept going back to the loo really often to keep checking and changing the toilet paper. I was petrified that the blood would leak into my skirt, which I think was a pale blue thin cotton skirt. Strangely I can't remember if I told my Mum what had happened or if she noticed, or if in fact I did leak blood onto my skirt. I think there may have been a bit on the car seat on the way home though. My Mum had seen I was 'developing' quite young so had already bought me sanitary towels which I had kept in my chest of drawers. Thinking about them now they seemed huge! (This was the mid 1980s.) I recall that the next day I told my Mum she wasn't to tell my sister about it at all – I didn't want her to know I had started my periods before her (she is 21 months older than me). I assume my Mum kept my secret – my sister and I have never talked about our first periods. Currently, some 25 years later, I don't like my periods, I find it a mess, annoying and I wish I didn't have them. I don't know if this is in any way connected to my first experience. Although I've charted my cycle in the past for a bit, I've started it again as I'm interested in the monthly pattern and changes in emotions, energy levels etc. I don't really have a problem with not liking my periods, and I feel ok about saying that even as a strong feminist! However, I use a Mooncup for most of the days, and try to use the Moon Pads at night, so it's not all bad! **Anon, Wales**

How do you feel after reading these stories?

How do they differ from your mums story (or Aunty's or Grandma's) or are they similar?

What do you think you would like to do when you start?

Who will you tell?

This booklet will give you lots of ideas of ways to celebrate but you might want to keep it private between you and your mum or your sister or maybe just a friend.

You could take the time right now to jot down some ideas or questions that have come up for you while reading these stories. Use this space.....

....

....

....

....

....

....

....

....

....

....

....

....

....

....

....

....

....

....

....

....

....

....

....

....

....

....

....

....

....

....

....

Celebrating your First Moon

The word 'celebrate' comes from an ancient Greek word 'melpo' which means to sing, dance and praise!

There are many ways to celebrate your first blood- here are a few suggestions-

Image: Menarche girls in the Moon Lodge

⋏ Have a RED PARTY! Invite your friends and all dress in red, decorate your home with red flowers, red cloths and eat red foods!

⋏ Have a 'pamper party' with your girlfriends, give each other facials, paint your toe nails, braid one another's hair- create a special girlie space to share your stories and perhaps read some of the ones in this book. Light a candle and share chocolate!   Create a ceremony - ask your mum and friends to help.

⋏ Talk to your mum about the steps to becoming a woman- is there something you'd like to help you to feel more grown up- to get your ears pierced, have your hair henna'd, or maybe redecorate your room? Chat some ideas over with your mum.

⋏ Give your period a name that creates affirmative thoughts about it; Moon Time, my moon, red moon, red tide, sacred cycle, moon cycle, my flow, my sacred time, my special time…..

⋏ Sew a soft red bag to keep your sanitary wear in

⋏ Give yourself a henna hand tattoo

⋏ Wear red knickers

⋏ Rest and relax- have a massage, do gentle yoga, sit by the fire, chant, meditate etc

⋏ Use soft comfortable cloth menstrual pads

⋏ Make a menstrual journal and record your dreams, visions, feelings during your Moon Time

⋏ Ask a your mum to cook your favourite meal

⋏ Create a peaceful place (your personal moon lodge/red tent)in your room, decorate it with fabrics and candles

⋏ Make a red silk dream pillow stuffed with relaxing herbs- only to use when you're bleeding! (sleep herbs are chamomile, lavender & lemon balm, for a Menstrual pillow use hops, rose petals, lavender and mugwort)

- Light red candles
- Choose special moon time bedding; red sheets or red flowers…
- Make a menstrual belt with leather strips and beads
- Drink red juice- grape, pomegranate, cherry, cranberry, beetroot
- Begin a women's circle; meet with friends and share your thoughts, feelings, and experiences of your cycle.
- Make a Moon Time Altar, choose special items that reflect your moon time and support the meditative qualities of this time of the month.
- Buy or make a special moon time necklace to wear when you bleed
- Turn off the TV, your mobile phone, the computer, the lights and sit in candle light
- Wear red lipstick!
- Read inspirational women's books
- Leave water out under the full moon, drink it and let the moons energy fill you
- Have someone braid/comb your hair
- Splash or spray yourself with Rose water
- Sing a song to Grandmother Moon
- Buy or make a special Moon Jar/container to keep your Moon Time things in, such as cloth pads/moon cup, jewellery, belts, altar items, fabrics, candles etc
- Paint or henna your nails
- Read books about the Goddess
- Henna your hair
- Write in your journal about what has happened in your life since your last bleeding time.
- Meditate on the moon
- Make a list of all the things in life that nourish you and make you happy
- Ask yourself- what is my image of a woman who embodies the sacred and holy time of menstruation?
- Stay in bed all day, sleep, dream & bleed!
- Wear a red skirt or dress
- Draw or paint, get creative- just see what comes
- Burn incense or sage and give thanks and a healing prayer- let the smoke carry your prayers in to the universe
- Your blood is sacred- dedicate your blood flow to healing.
- Say a prayer of gratitude when you begin to bleed each month; thanking your body for connecting you to the rhythm of life.
- Anoint yourself with scented oils

- ⅄ Wear red clothes!
- ⅄ Eat chocolate!
- ⅄ Buy a red hot water bottle
- ⅄ Make a belly pouch- to keep your hot water bottle at your belly (or use a scarf)
- ⅄ Drum, rattle, sing, chant, then in the quiet listen to your inner voice- ask it for guidance
- ⅄ Play with divination/oracle cards
- ⅄ Gather your friends for a pamper evening, give each other face masks, foot rubs and eat lovely snacks!
- ⅄ Rub warm oil on your lower back and belly
- ⅄ Bathe in rose petals
- ⅄ Make a red hot water bottle cover to ease your cramps
- ⅄ Tell your friends and family you are on your Moon Time
- ⅄ Give thanks to your body and tell her you love her!
- ⅄ Go for a night time walk and see what phase the moon is in. make a note in your journal and compare moon phases each month.
- ⅄ Or use some of the bonding ideas on page 19

Written in 1998 added to when inspired further by 105 Ways to Celebrate your Menstruation by Kami Mc Bride

Image: Sacred space created at a women's gathering on Samhien (Halloween)

A young woman's celebration:

My Menarche Ceremony at Sacred Arts Camp *by Ro Ocean 2006*

My Menarche Ceremony this year was truly beautiful. I just wish every girl could experience what I did. The sweat lodge the night before the ceremony was just as important as the actual thing, as it cleansed your body to give that sense of readiness to the experience.

Image: Ro in the Moon-Lodge

Just before dusk us girls and our moon mothers gathered by the roaring fire and where smudged with sage before entering the small dome tent which was the sweat lodge. I felt nervous seeing as this was the first sweat lodge I'd ever been to. As our eyes adjusted to the blackness, seven stones were produced and put into a pit in the centre of the circle we had formed. Then we sang 'we are sacred' into the sticky atmosphere to the beat of a boran. We went round the circle saying what we wanted to let go of and what we wanted to bring with us on our sacred journey to womanhood.

The air grew unbearably hot and when it was time to go back to reality I felt as if I'd just come out of a swimming pool! Coming out of the dark was like being reborn- an experience I will treasure for ever and ever and ever!

On the day of the ceremony, I made my way to the moon lodge to meet my moon mother, Chrystia and change into my white clothes. I was glad to have the company of the other girls although I knew everyone was there to celebrate and support me.

Once we were ready, the maidens came to lead us to the big top where we entered through a beautiful ash tree arch. Then we were smudged with sage by the crones in their gorgeous black and purple robes and shouted our names into the immense circle of women and girls.

When they sung to us songs old and new, I felt more comfortable as I know most of the old songs from past menarche's so I sang along.

Then we changed into our daring red dresses back in the moon lodge and came out to something very unexpected!

We walked between two lines of men and boys with their backs to us; drumming random beats every now and again with minutes between each singular beat. The energy in that path so incredibly powerful- you'd really have to experience it to understand it!

Once we were in the big top again, while the women danced and sung to us, my moon mother whispered my moon name to me and handed me a precious card. I felt honoured to have so much attention paid to me!

After we had witnessed belly dancing and listened to a story, we turned our heads to hear the questions of the crones who were guarding the gates; "should we let these men in?" "Do they respect and honour us as sisters?" the men were let in and they stood in front of us girls who were in a line with our moon mothers by our side. Then the men sang 'we honour you', once for every girl being celebrated. Then the moon fathers stepped forward to crown their moon daughters one by one.

Image: Menarche girls wait to be crowned by their moon fathers

I was proud of my luscious crown; it was decorated with small flowers and two red roses at the side- in fact, it is sitting on my hearth right this minute.

How are you feeling about it?
This page is a journal page to explore how you feel about your period- or getting your period if you haven't started yet.

When you start your period you might look back and notice you have been feeling 'different' for a while- perhaps you've been emotional- maybe you've been quiet and weepy or feisty and angry, you might have just felt a bit 'weird' or not yourself.
When it comes you may feel nervous or excited that its happened to you, all girls feel different.

If you have started note here the date:

My Moon Time (period) came on..................

I was at...

I felt...
....
....
....
....
....
....
....
....
....
....
....
....
....
....
....
....
....

If you haven't started your Moon Time yet- you'll still be thinking and feeling a lot about it- so use this space to write how you are feeling and maybe some ideas about how you might want to celebrate.

You might want to write about how its been for you if your friends have already started and how it has been for them?

....

....

....

....

....

....

....

....

....

....

....

....

....

....

....

....

....

....

....

....

....

....

....

....

....

....

....

....

....

....

Bonding ideas for Mother and Daughter

This stage in your daughters life often means a lot less time with family, and more time spent with friends! To keep your relationship strong why not choose a couple of these activities to do on a regular basis? Talk thought them and see which ones appeal to you both.

♥ Make a 'date', make sure at some point each week you make a date to spend time together- it could be to go shopping for something special or just for school shoes, or to go to a cafe for cake and tea, maybe you will do some of the other ideas listed below! Make it a date just for the two of you.

♥ Read a 'womens' book together- like the Red Tent by Anita Diamant or How to be a Woman by Caitlin Moran. Have discussions about what you have read.

♥ Introduce your daughter to healing herbal teas – why not have a sacred tea ceremony and really take the time to tune in to each step of the tea making and then the herb you are drinking. Tell her about its healing qualities.

♥ Make a 'talking stick' together and promise one another that you will listen and be attentive to each other whenever is is used. A Talking Stick can be made from anything- a decorated stick, or even a pencil, or rattle, a shell or a stone- whatever you feel is right for you.

♥ Create a moon journal together – you could include the moons phases as well as your personal 'moon time'. Record your moods and emotions. (for a 'ready made' Moon Journal see www.moontimes.co.uk Cycle Charting Journal)

♥ Cook something special together- it might be a favourite meal or just baking a cake! Maybe try something really different like making your own chocolate or some fun fairy cakes! (yoni fairy cakes pictured!)

♥ Make a sacred space. Help your daughter find a space in her room where she can create a special space. (in Steiner Schools they have nature tables- this is like a Moon Time table!) She can include shells, crystals, treasures, candles, figures, photographs or any of her special treasures! See article Be Creative with your Cycle for other ideas

♥ Share your stories with your daughter, your fist period, how you and her father met, your first love, her birth (or adoption), memories from being a teenager. Show her photos of yourself at her age- let her know and see you were once young too!

♥ Share your PMT tips with her, tell her how your own moon time is each month, if its easy and painless tell her that, if you have suffered cramps, mood swings, bloatedness, heavy flow- whatever, tell her! Be real! If you don't have any tips then read this booklet with her and discuss the tips in here.

♥ Start a Mother and Daughters group;invite some of your daughters friends and their mums over- perhaps once a month on a dark or full moon. You could begin with informal chats and sharing food and discuss future topics such as sharing first period stories, discuss inspiring womens books, alternatives in sanitary wear, go for a moon lit walk together, bring your favourite music and have a dance, have a pamper eve- do shoulder massages or foot rubs, make your own beauty products- such as avocado face masks, have a pad making evening- or just share a craft idea! Make it fun for all of you.

Image- weaving women at Imbolc, making Brigids Crosses

Menarche- a Journey into Womanhood

Rites of passage have begun to reappear in our society as we recognise the importance of honouring our young people and guiding them gently into adulthood. Ceremonies, vision quests, men's and women's lodges, rite of passage courses, festivals and camps are becoming more and more popular!

I have been working with women and their daughters for many years supporting them in celebrating their rite of passage. For girls there is a clear signal that their journey into womanhood has begun- with the start of their periods. The first period is known as Menarche; tribal traditions have celebrated Menarche for thousands of years- some rituals including the whole tribe, others more private among close women friends and family, some quite extreme- including genital mutilation, cutting, scarring and tattooing, other more gentle – being fed, massaged and sung to.

I believe how a young woman is guided through this experience can affect her for the rest of her life! Ask your women friends how they celebrated their first period- sadly for the majority of women it was ignored, shamed, at best explained clinically and 'gifts' of huge pads (sometimes huge tampons!) often terrified young girls! The menstrual cycle is a crucial element in the balance of the body, mind, spirit connection for a woman; this needs to be taught from an early age so when her cycle begins (signs can begin as early as 1 year before her blood flow) she can feel proud and excited to begin her journey of power!

I eagerly anticipated my daughters Menarche- I'd been working for a number of years around menstruation and creating pretty cloth pads for the women on my courses and their friends.

My period had started when I was 11- but Tabitha was a different build to me; very petite, so I wasn't expecting her to start as early as I had. But soon after her 12th birthday I began to notice a 'cycle' to her mood swings- even chocolate cravings for a few days each month! Other physical signs were night sweats for a couple of nights, slight cramps as she ovulated (which she presumed was a tummy ache), breaking out in spots….all the usual. She'd have a few days when she felt unattractive, hated all her clothes- they didn't fit or look right! And she would cry at the slightest thing. After about 6 months of these 'symptoms' one morning she came in my room as she had bled in the night and her sheets needed changing and she needed cleaning up! She was happy to have finally started but eager to wash and change.

I ran her a bath with rose bath salts and a sprinkle of lavender oil, re-made her bed while she soaked and prepared her a hot water bottle. She had the day off school and I excitedly gave her a set of pads I had made and mentioned the celebration I had planned; we would invite our girl friends over, dress in red, have red foods and drinks, bless her with gifts, songs and create a special ceremony just for her!

Oh, the look on her face, "Oh no mum!" she really wasn't up for it!

So I had to put my excitement, my plans, my expectations to one side and listen to what she wanted.

We celebrated quite traditionally; a meal out at her favourite restaurant with her best friend and a gift of a new pair of earrings!

For the next year or so she suffered from very heavy, painful periods- she was lucky that they were very regular from the start so we knew when it would come, but it concerned me that her flow was so heavy as she was still such a slight build of a woman- and vegetarian- so I worried about her iron levels and how draining this heavy loss was making her feel. She was flooding her disposable pads at school and was constantly worried about bleeding on to her clothes. Although she loved her cloth pads- and preferred them to disposables, even finding them better at absorbing her heavy flow- but she wasn't yet confident enough to use them at school, so we opted for the organic cotton throwaways as a compromise.

We visited a naturopath who recommended a liver cleanse drink to take for a couple of months pre-menstrually. Amazingly this totally balanced her flow (I joined her in the cleanse and felt its positive effects- more energy, clear skin and my periods became lighter! Even now I continue to do the cleanse every 6 months or so.) And her period has been 'normal' ever since!

And much to my joy I eventually got my wish to celebrate Tabitha with my community of women when she was 15!

I had been taking part in the Menarche Ceremony preparation at Sacred Arts Camp for a couple of years- running workshops with the young women and their mothers who were taking part; teaching them about charting their cycle, making moon necklaces, decorating red and white candles...

This particular year Tabitha came to camp with her friend who was keen to take part...so Tabi agreed to join her, choosing my best friend Nicho to be her 'Moon Mother' and my husband Tom as her 'Moon Father'.

What I love about this ceremony is that it is open to any woman who hadn't been celebrated at her menarche- as well as all the girls who have recently begun to bleed. So ages of those taking part can be from 10-40! It also involves the men, the grandmothers, the very young girls- anyone who wants to join in can have a role.

Image: Women chant and Drum during a menarche celebration

All week women meet in my moon lodge tipi to co-create the ceremony – deciding what songs will be sung, what dances to dance, finding musicians, collecting red and white clothes for the women taking part, choosing who will take which role....

Meanwhile the young women choose a Moon Mother who will attend the ceremony with them holding their hand and reassuring them, bringing them a gift, helping them to get ready, they might share blood stories with them and as part of the ceremony they dream them a 'moon name' the night before the ritual. Many Moon Mother/Moon Daughter relationships continue years after the ceremony- even though girls may choose a woman who they only see once a year at camp! They also choose a Moon Father – someone older who can be another 'wise father figure' in their life and who will also make them a crown of leaves and flowers for the ceremony! The Moon Fathers have a powerful role in the ritual- bringing in the male energy.

Other men of the community get involved; they will meet to prepare- perhaps creating a song for the ceremony as well as sharing stories with each other about men's traditions and honouring women! Their part in the ceremony is to 'guard' the sacred ceremonial space by dressing as 'warriors' and walking around the outside perimeter whilst drumming and chanting.

Once the Moon Fathers enter (after being challenged by the 'Grandmothers' -menopausal women) all the men will join the ceremony.

IMAGE: full tent!

The ritual begins with the decorating of the big top- draping it in whatever cloths and sheets we have, flowers are placed in vases and jars, an entrance is made from willow and flowers, (the entrance is guarded by the wise grandmothers who welcome the girls in) lighting candles and incense and raising the energy by singing and chanting while we decorate and smudge ourselves with white sage!

All the women dress up- white if you haven't begun to bleed yet, red if you're a bleeding woman and black/purple for the menopausal women- although some women prefer just to wear any 'dressy up' clothes they have brought!

While this is happening the young women get ready with their moon mums in the moon lodge, being anointed with sacred water and dressing in white with a white ribbon in their hair.

Each year the ceremony is slightly different, this year, watching my daughter take part- and also taking part myself as her best friends Moon Mother was an emotional time for me! I don't recall too much as I spent the ceremony on 'auto pilot' through my tears!

Walking in to a big top filled with 200+ women singing is a powerful experience! They sang and danced for the girls and their Moon Mothers, and then we left to change the girls from white to red- as each one left the space they turned and called out their name symbolizing leaving their 'girl- child' part of them self behind.

While we helped them change in the moon lodge, the ceremony continued with the passing of the 'Yoni Cushion' as a talking stick – as it passed each woman they spoke 3 words to summarise their bleeding experience- words like 'connected, pain, loss, renewal and even –I'm not pregnant'!

After that songs and chants are shared until the young women re-enter- dressed in beautiful red clothes. The singing continues in honour of them and then there is the ceremonial hair cutting- once again symbolising the letting go of their childhood- the hair with the white ribbon is cut away and they are anointed with a red ochre crescent moon on their forehead- to remind them of their moon connection and the rhythm and flow of the moon. They drank from the sacred goblet (blackcurrant juice!) and then the Moon Mothers step forward to bless them with gifts and their new 'moon names' are whispered to them.

Now is the time for the men to enter! The Grandmothers had been guarding the entrance the whole time and now step back to allow the men in- first they were challenged 'Do you come in to this space with love and respect for your sisters?' To which of course they answered yes!

The 'Moon Fathers' stepped forward and crowned their Moon Daughters, as the rest of the men sang their gift song they had composed.

In return- our gift to the men for protecting our space was to share with them a blood mystery story- told by one of our amazing storytellers.

After that the musicians played, joined by the drummers and it was time to celebrate and dance the evening away!!

The young women left with their Moon Mums to go back to the moon lodge and have chocolate cake and ground after the ritual. Later that night (it was a full moon) we had a women's sweat lodge- the perfect ending to a wonderful day!

IMAGE: Tabitha is crowned by her Moon Father & step father Tom

Tabitha told me afterwards that although she had been really nervous and unsure about taking part, she was really glad she did and loved how 'special' she had felt!

Tabitha has been such a joy to me- such an amazing young woman who has embraced supporting me in my work, she has challenged school friends, teachers and colleagues to look at their menstruation differently and use earth and body-friendly sanitary wear. She even accompanied me to the USA to attend the Red Web Conference in 2007!
Tabitha is now 23, she works in fashion and is a DJ and film maker.

To find out more about Sacred Arts Camp see www.sacredartscamp.org

Liver cleanse:

Supporting the liver has amazing results with menstrual problems!
Below is a Liver Tonic drink:
1 tablespoon Olive Oil
Juice of ½ lemon
1 clove of garlic
1 glass of Apple juice
1/8th inch of Ginger
Blend and drink each morning for 3 days, then reduce to 1 morning a week until menstruation. Avoid dairy products pre-menstrually.

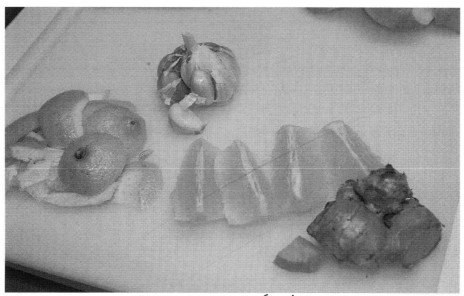
Image: ingredients for cleanse

The health and vitality of every organ, gland, and cell are dependent upon the liver. Even our intelligence, attitudes, emotions and vitality are largely related to the liver. Our ability to repel disease or recover from disease is very much associated with this incredible organ. The liver, along with the heart and brain, are the most important organs in our bodies. However, even the heart and the brain are dependent on the liver. No one can be healthy without a strong, clean liver.

"As women we are the keepers of a wisdom that restores balance … The women's mysteries are not only to do with fertility and birth. They also teach the lessons of blood, pain, loss, the shadow, decay and death, which are also a part of life on earth". Michelle Royce /Spiraldancer

The Native Americans believe the dreams women have when they are on their Moon Time can bring important messages- for the woman and her community. Use this space to write about any Moon Time dreams you have had.

....
....
....
....
....
....
....
....
....
....
....
....
....
....
....
....
....
....
....
....
....
....
....
....
....
....
....
....
....
....

Whats going on in your body?
Understanding our Cycles

"Listening… adds a richness and connection to life…… The tendencies in the ovulatory phase of the cycle are more outer focussed, linear, left brain, feeling fairly clear and productive, with plenty of energy for others. As we move into the menstrual phase of the cycle women tend to become more inner focussed. The transition to this inner state is often signalled by feelings of irritability, anger, overwhelm, greater dreaminess and vagueness. The people around us often feel more like an irritant. Opposites are amplified. For example you may experience feeling driven one moment and then flip into it's opposite, becoming drifty and dreamy the next. A feeling of purposefulness may fall away to be replaced by a questioning about one's life…Equally there are moments of spaciousness and even peacefulness (if you're not too busy), passionate feeling, heightened intuition, psychic ability and strong dreaming. The single most dominant characteristic of this phase is sensitivity." Alexandra Pope

There are 2 major phases in our monthly cycle- ovulation and menstruation.

Coming in to ovulation we are usually outgoing, energetic and creative. Where as coming up to our bleeding we can feel more reflective and introspective. These 'extremities' are part of the dance of your monthly cycle and change from month to month.

Keep a record of your own cycle in a notebook, diary or using a moon dial or mandala (see next page!), just taking a few minutes each day to connect to your cycle and yourself can empower you immensely. Notice what phase the moon is in when you bleed and ovulate and notice how this changes from month to month.

Keeping a journal is all about noticing- not judging. Noticing the variations in our moods, impulses, our communication, state of mind, health, diet, intentions, sexuality, feelings and much more! As you go through this journal you will begin to connect with your unique cycle and see what patterns emerge, you will deepen your experience of your own rhythms.

Some words you may want to use: proud, weepy, special, bored, lonely,beautiful, sad, creative, angry, weird, dreamy, hurt, confused, clumsy, peaceful, comfortable, frustrated, tense, confident, loving, hungry, loved, dreamy, angry, full, vibrant, irritated, unloved, nervous, overwhelmed, loving, achey, relaxed, playful, funny, mad, happy, inspired, embarrassed, shy, energetic, at ease, lively, teary,rejected, friendly, thankful, joyful, annoyed, refreshed, sorry, cleansed…

The Monthly Cycle

This diagram shows a 'regular' 28 day cycle....we'll break it down on the next pages.

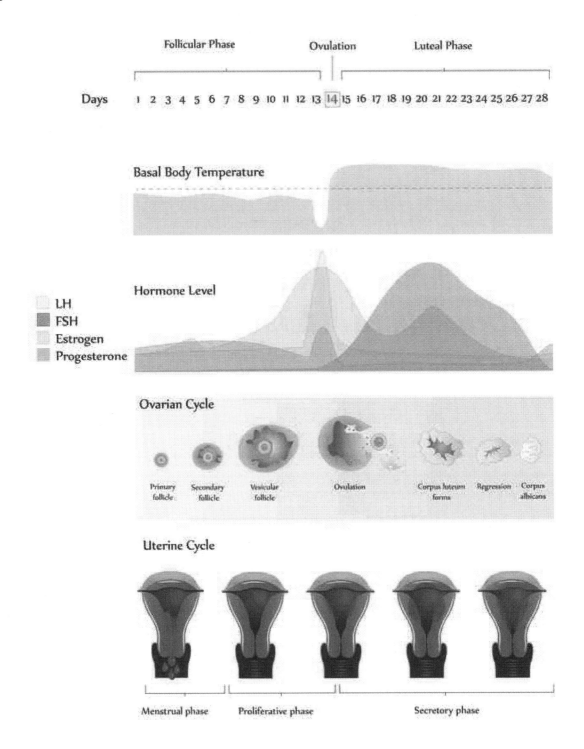

Once your periods start, you are 'on a cycle' like the seasons of the year and the moon! Have you noticed how nature moves in cycles?

There are 5 hormonal phases we will be looking at:

Bleeding; time for resting, our bleeding time can be anything from 3-7 days. The first day of bleeding is day 1 of your cycle.

Pre ovulation; the extrovert side of us comes out before we ovulate, this phase can last 3 days up to 2 weeks.

Ovulation; the creative time of our cycle when our egg is released, this lasts 3 days and occurs 14/16 days before your bleeding time. Hormonally and biologically speaking this is the 'main event' of the month!

Post ovulation; the time of evaluation, a time for reflection in the week between ovulation and before bleeding begins.

Pre bleeding; the heightened sensitivity phase the week before our bleeding time.

As you cycle though each phase your hormones are like a roller coaster going up to ovulation, peaking and then travelling down to the premenstrual phase.

"Give yourself time to tune in and reclaim your cyclic nature. Write a short journal entry everyday. The rewards for doing this are beyond measure. You'll feel connected to life in a whole new way, with increased respect for yourself and your magnificent hormones." Dr Christiane Northrup

Notice how within the four weeks of your cycle, your moods change, your feelings towards your physical appearance differ, how you communicate changes, your perspective of the world around you alters, this is all because of your wonderful hormones, rising and falling like the ocean waves!

Lets start looking at your cycle with your bleeding phase-

The week you begin to bleed your intuition is strong; you feel like withdrawing from the world, you want to be alone and often if you don't get your 'me' time you'll feel moody with those around you.

This is the Dark Moon – Wise Woman Menstruation Phase; You are a wise woman, no longer focused on others, you seeks solitude, others may ask you for guidance – you welcome them. You are able to be completely honest, as you hold the wisdom; you teach and share stories with those who will listen!

Does your family support you in your retreat? Do you have a "new vision" of your life; is some of it falling apart? Are you bursting with creative energy, wanting to give birth to ideas and projects?

The Wise Woman can be bitter and angry if she did not complete the tasks of the previous phases of the cycle, making it difficult to let go, she may isolate herself and blame others for her misfortune, her rage can be fiery; her sadness deep. The Wise Womans' responsibility is to share her knowledge; she returns the seed of vision back to the maiden, for within her is a lively girl and loving woman. We lose so much of ourselves; within and without, when we lose connection with the wisdom of the Wise Woman.

"Your feeling may be one of not knowing what to do; the line of feminine teachings may have been lost to you. And I say, the Mother's truth is always within us; be willing to discover it within yourself." Brooke Medicine Eagle

At this point in your cycle Testosterone is released from the ovaries and the adrenal glands, it gives us a bit of 'get up and go'!
During your bleeding time Oxytocin levels peak- it causes the uterus to contact and creates the shedding of the uterine lining. Progesterone drops dramatically also triggering your bleeding.

Oxytocin is the LOVE hormone, when levels peak women feel more inspired, clear and 'connected'. It is also triggered when we fall in love, when we spend time with friends and are intimate with others.
Research shows that dream activity increases during this pre- menstrual phase and images about death and loss are common.
Menstruation is a time for letting go, resting, preparation time for the month ahead. During bleeding time many women feel the need to seclude themselves from the world and rest.

"The flow of blood can be thought of as the monthly 'clean out' of not only the body but the mind and spirit….a good time to spend at home- just relaxing and doing things related to letting go and clearing out" Dr Christiane Northrup.

Delve in to your Dark Phase; it is a time for rebirth. Listen to your inner wisdom.

On a spiritual level the menstrual phase brings heightened vision and sensitivity. In the Native American Tradition (and many other tribal traditions) women would retreat to their moon lodge during their menses, they would sing, chant, meditate and bring back any visions and dreams they had to the tribe. Many important prophecies throughout the history of time have come from menstruating women. The oldest Greek Oracle in history- Delphi was ruled by the Moon Goddess- Delphi means spiritual womb.

"Among our dreaming peoples, the most prophetic dreams and visions (of the coming of the white peoples and other such almost incomprehensible changes) were brought to the people through the Moon Lodge." Brooke Medicine Eagle

"In the ruddy shade of the red tent, the menstrual tent, they ran their fingers through my curls, repeating the escapades of their youths, the sagas of their childbirths. Their stories were like offerings of hope and strength poured out before the Queen of Heaven, only these gifts were not for any god or goddess - but for me." The Red Tent by Anita Diamant

After bleeding you enter your Maiden, Waxing Moon Phase, you have new dynamic energy, it is a renewal time, ideal for planting ideas. The shift from bleeding to ovulation is noticeable around days 6-8.

What will you do with the rising energy of your upcoming ovulation?
"Many women find that they are at their 'best' from the onset of their menstrual cycle until ovulation. Their energy is out going and upbeat. They are filled with enthusiasm and new ideas" Dr Christiane Northrup.

You are the maiden - a young woman, pure of heart, full of love and curiosity, experimenting with life, having new experiences. In you are the seeds of all potential: all possibilities are within.
You do not allow others beliefs or needs limit you The mystery of life is your inspiration. Unto yourself you are whole, you are, by herself complete.

The Maidens negative traits are a tendency to become lost in her world, becoming self destructive, deaf to her inner voice and wisdom. Sometimes she is dutiful, pleasing others in order to receive approval to boost her self worth. If she has not yet developed her sense of self she may lose herself.
She must find herself, her voice, gain inner knowledge through her own ideas, thoughts, values and purpose. She needs to have a vision for her life. This is hard without the encouragement to explore and believe in herself, especially if other people's opinions take on more power than her own journey of self discovery.

The Ovulating Mother-Full Moon Phase- You devote yourself to things outside yourself, you birth creation; not the birth of a child - but all possibilities of creation; producing art, gaining knowledge, pursuit of a profession, anything that allows the "birthing" of creative energy within.

Approximately 11 days after day 1 of your bleeding, your oestrogen begins to peak, you become aware of your attractiveness and how you present yourself, you radiate love and share your expanded creativity with friends. Oestrogen is produced in the ovaries and is the 'plentiful' hormone in women! It triggers ovulation and also helps regulate our sleep patterns.

How are you aware of your physical signs of fertility? What is most noticeable?

During puberty it is Oestrogen that changes our sweat glands, vaginal secretions and triggers breast development. In pregnancy it again triggers breast and uterus growth, and changes in the vagina and cervix. Its departure at peri-menopause causes hot flashes and ends our menstrual cycle.

Ovulation Mother is selfless, her love is unconditional. She must choose her path and commit to it. She takes the virgins dreams and manifests them as her choice. The strong Self developed as a maiden now becomes humbled in service, selflessness and unconditional love. This is her choice, not duty.
As the Mother is depended on to nurture and protect, she has the power to abuse and abandon, control, criticise and reject. If her strong sense of self was not developed in the virgin she may lose herself, resenting the caring role, denying herself and becoming a martyr. If she has a healthy self awareness then spiritual awareness may be discovered as the ego is humbled by love, service and creation. She is on the path to finding the wisdom of the Wise Woman.

Oestrogen begins to drop after its peak at approx day 12 has triggered ovulation. By day 15 its levels have dropped below progesterone level. With the release of the egg progesterone is secreted by the follicle. Testosterone peaks with ovulation along with Oxytocin.

The spirit of Oestrogen is closely connected to our feminine side; it feels great! It's ebbing and flowing is closely related to our moods and energy balance, our feelings around socialising- our need to be with others. It increases when we 'fall in love'! Its release improves the parts of the brain associated with emotions, communication, study and intuition.
Ovulation dreams are reported to include babies, eggs, and jewels, fragile and precious objects.
"At mid cycle we are naturally more receptive to others and to new ideas....The [hormonal] surge that accompanies ovulation may be the biological basis for increased mental and emotional creative receptivity experienced at

ovulation….our male dominated society values this phase very highly, and we internalise it as a 'good' stage of our cycle." Dr Christiane Northrup

After ovulation your Good Witch/Enchantress Waxing Moon Phase comes into play! You may feel impatient with things that seem pointless you become less patient as you descend from your high point of fertility. It is a time of letting go, looking at what is working well in your life. You will become more perceptive to the connection between your physical and your emotional sides.

Now Progesterone kicks in, produced by the ovaries, it stimulates uterine lining growth for nurturing an embryo should one be conceived! It feeds the womb with proteins and starches. The drop in Progesterone and Oestrogen just before bleeding causes the uterine lining to shed- creating our bleeding time. Progesterone slows, calms and relaxes us; she can stimulate creativity but also make us intolerant, contemplative, explosive…..She tries to create quietness in our body so it can connect with the effects of our ovulation!
Testosterone and Oxytocin decrease. Oestrogen rises after the drop at ovulation and stays at a constant level into pre-bleeding.

What reflections of yourself, your shadow /darker side, are now present? Are you able to embrace this side of yourself?
What will you do to support yourself as you need to withdraw from the outer world? Are there any communications you need to speak now? Are you ready and wanting to bleed and let go?

Now begins the **Warrior/ Sorceress Waning to New Moon Phase**. Premenstually Oestrogen drops off to its lowest point and bleeding begins (levels rise with pregnancy). Progesterone has peaked and drops off steadily. Oxytocin peaks and stimulates womb contractions. Testosterone kicks in during this phase.

DANCE LIKE THE MAIDEN, LAUGH LIKE THE MOTHER, THINK LIKE THE CRONE

"When I am premenstrual the things that make me teary are the things most important to me, things I know tune me in to my power and my deepest truths. My increased sensitivity feels like a gift of insight. I don't become angry, though if I did I would pay attention and not chalk it up to my 'stupid' hormones." Dr Christiane Northrup

And so you bleed again completing your monthly cycle.

Using a Moon Dial /Menstrual Mandala

When you begin your next period, find out what phase the moon is in, write the date against this bit of the moon and make a few notes about how your feeling, or dreaming or bleeding you may want to use different colours for different moods - try to do this for a few months and notice if there's a pattern. Some questions you could ask yourself- do I want to be alone? Am I letting go of anything? How am I dressing? Do I feel attractive? Do I feel more sensitive to some things? Does my intuition feel stronger than usual? (see moon dial associations for more ideas)

If you count day 1 as the first day of your period you should notice that around day 14 you will be ovulating- should notice a sticky patch in your knickers! I know I usually feel crappy, crabby, bloated and spotty the day before my period- it'd reassuring to know that its only cos I'm premenstrual! As soon as I begin to bleed I feel fine! Phew!

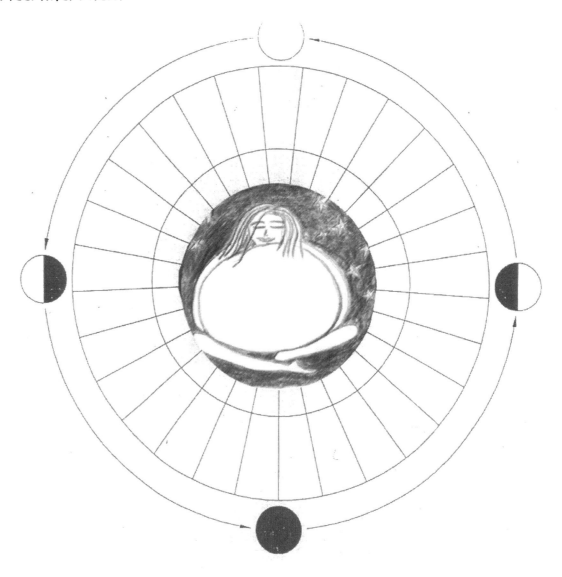

The Connection to the Moon

We know the tides of the oceans are caused by the magnetic pull of the moon. Scientific evidence shows that our biological cycles are connected to the moon and the tides, they work together with the electromagnetic fields of our body and affect our physiological responses.

The average woman's menstrual cycle is 29.5 days- the same length of the moons cycle. It takes 29.5 days for the moon to wax from new to full and wane from full to new again.

There are many parallels between the moons cycle and our menstrual cycle; the introspective dark energy of the new moon is similar to the time of menstruation and the outward fullness of the full moon is similar to ovulation.

Research has shown that women living without artificial lights (home lighting, street lights etc have created an unnatural disconnection to our natural relationship with the light of the sun and moon) and who don't eat foods that contain artificial hormones naturally bleed at the dark/new moon and ovulate with the full moon.

Many Tribal peoples refer to the moon as 'Grandmother' and admire her as an ancient wise one. Keeping track of the moon in your journal may invite some of the wisdom of Grandmother Moon in to your life!

If you use a journal or diary why not draw the moon on each journal page to help you connect more with her ebbing and flowing?

A note about the Thirteenth Moon

There are Thirteen Moon Cycles in one solar year, The Mayans used a thirteen month calendar- when the patriarchal Gregorian Solar Calendar was created the Mayans said women had been 'robbed of their moon and their power.'

"Transformation begins;
the wheel of life turns
around the centre of spirit.
It dances and flows with the rhythm of my cycle
within me.
Turning, ever turning.
The Cycle of Life"
So watch for that month that there are 2 full moons and perhaps you have 2 bleeds.

Be Creative with your Cycle *by Dominique Sakoilsky*

Our bleeding time is a time to turn inwards– its nice to have a special place to go (this is where the tribal moon lodges came from)...here's some ideas for you! Give yourself a space, especially for your bleeding time, where you can be comfortable, relax, turn inwards and connect to yourself and the earth.
Some ideas to create a space for moon time:
Cushions, pillows, blankets.
Tarot cards, runes.
Pencils, paints, pens, paper – to make notes, pictures, poems, dreams.
A drum.
Goddess figures.
Special shells, stones, crystals.
Candles, incense and smudge stick (sage for cleansing & protecting, sweet grass for spirit and mugwort for visions.)
Oil burner (chamomile and lavender essential oils to relax.)
Massage oil.
Don't over clutter your space or make yourself feel over stimulated, bleeding time is a time of reflection and inner connectedness which flows out to connect all around.
Often, making things helps to still the mind and help us deeper in to the wisdom of our bodies.
Dream pillows stuffed with lavender flowers and mugwort, decorated especially by you makes a beautiful bleeding time gift to yourself, or making a prayer stick: choose a stick that appeals to you and wrap threads of different colours and textures all around it, add other decorations, such as beads, crystals– anything that feels right. Smudging and chanting while you work will help open your heart and put healing intent and prayers into your stick. You could keep all your sticks from each month and burn them together in a ritual to release your prayers or burn it each time you make one.
Treading a necklace; putting healing and sacred energy in to it, connecting to your cycling nature when you wear it. Choose beads that relate to your different cycle phases and the moons cycle.
Touch your menstrual blood or paint with it, how does that feel? Does it bring up feelings of how you relate to your blood, the way it looks, feels, smells?
All these suggestions can help you open the doorway to your intuition and enter your Dream Time.

A Moon Dial to photocopy!

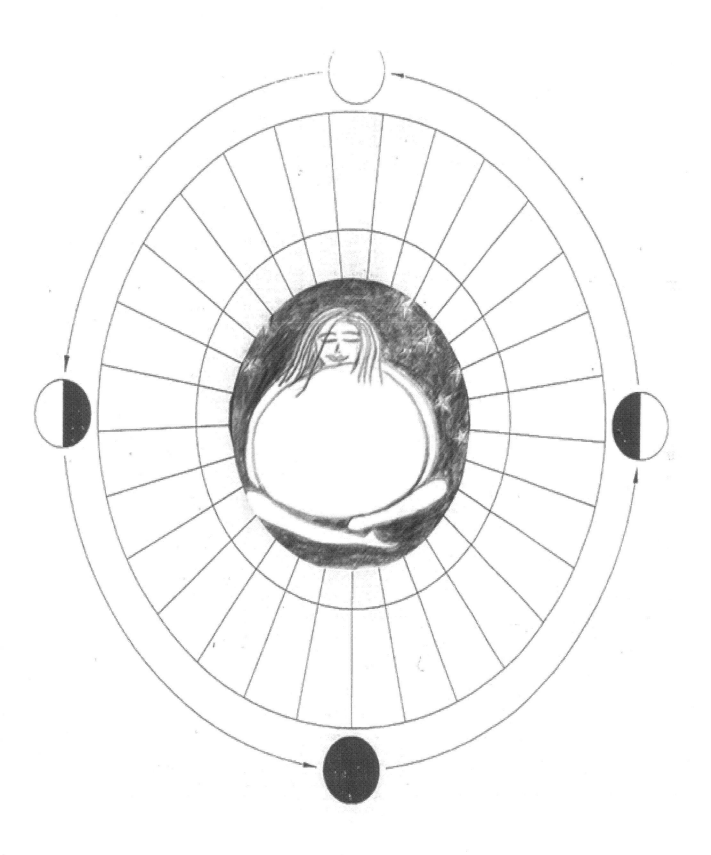

Moon Diary Ideas....things you may wish to write about

Cycle Phase- which phase are you in? What day are you on? (day 1 is the first day of your period) draw pictures or colour code your phases- you might choose red for bleeding, purple for after bleeding, yellow for pre-ovulation, blue for ovulation, green for post ovulation, pink for the time before bleeding...

Moon Phase- use a moon chart to see where the moon is, draw a picture or make a note of its phase. Where is your cycle in relation to the moon phase? Do you feel different in your creativity during the full and new moons? What do you feel when you menstruate or ovulate on or around the full and new moons. Notice the intensity of your bleeding and ovulation during the moons phases. Make a note if you have done any moon watching or spent time in nature. Do you feel any connection with the moon, the tides and your body?

Physical changes-make a note of all things physical; breast tenderness, how much exercise and sleep you are getting, food cravings etc
How are you dressing? Style- romantic, comfy, practical, sensual, glitzy, girly, tom boy...? Colours- bright or neutral?

Moods- how you've been feeling generally as well as any specific events. Do you feel joyful, at peace, anxious, angry, fearful, loving, connected....do you feel emotions in specific parts of your body?

Dreams- any insights, coincidences, dreams, connections to your spiritual self. Do you recall any vivid dreams? Have you been listening to your gut and trusting your intuition?

Energy- your energy levels, including your sexual and creative energy. How is your general energy? Tired, productive, retreating, self-motivated, vibrant, contemplative, anxious.....?
Are you feeling connected or disconnected to yourself? Are you irritable and in need of space? How are you expressing yourself...painting, dancing, singing, gardening, running, yoga, exercise, poetry, cooking....? Do you have impulses...to clean, organise, create a ritual?
Needs- are there specific things you needed today, did they get met? Was there something that stood out today? Something important that needed addressing?

Periods Around The World *from onewoman.com*

Here in the West we do little to honour a girl when she begins to menstruate, while in other cultures it is more of a big deal. Other cultures also think about periods differently than we do- here's some information-

NEW GUINEA   Among the Arapesh people, who live in New Guinea, there is a traditional celebration of a girl's first menstruation. It takes place in her husband's home (Arapesh girls are married before they begin to menstruate), but her family takes part in it too. Her brothers build her a fine menstrual hut, a temporary home, where she sits with her legs crossed. Her woven arm and leg bands are removed, and the things she carries with her every day are taken away, so that she will have a fresh start on life. She stays in the hut for three days, fasting. She drinks no water and eats no food. On the third day she comes out and an uncle makes little decorative cuts on her shoulders and buttocks. This is called scarification, and is considered a beautiful way to decorate the body.

INDIA   In the South of India and in Ceylon, the Brahmin community performs a traditional ritual to celebrate the beginning of menstruation called Samati Sadang. The hope is that the girl will lead a fertile life. The girl sits on banana leaves and eats raw egg flavoured with ginger oil and then she is given a bath in milk. When this ritual is over, the whole family comes together to feast and celebrate her becoming a mature female. When a Nayar girl of India begins her period, she may be secluded, and then visited by neighbour women and dressed in new clothes. She usually will begin wearing a sari, a woman's dress, at this time. Later she and her friends will take a ceremonial bath, and then go to a feast where "drums are beaten and shouts of joy are given."

ANCIENT IRELAND   In ancient Celtic story called "The Cattle Raid of Cuchalainn" there was a beautiful, powerful warrior queen named Maeve. She led her people in battle against the legendary hero Cuchulainn. According to the story, Queen Maeve was an equal opponent for this great hero. The only reason she lost the battle against him is because her period began and she had to get out of her chariot to take care of it. When she did, Cuchalainn snuck up behind Queen Maeve and captured her. The spot on which she bled was forever after known as "Maeve's Foul Place."

IVORY COAST   An elder (an older, respected member of the community) of the Beng people of Africa's Ivory Coast explains what his people believe about menstruation: "Menstrual blood is special because it carries in it a living being. It works like a tree. Before bearing fruit, a tree must first bear flowers. Menstrual blood is like the flower: it must emerge before the fruit - the baby - can be born. Childbirth is like a tree finally bearing its fruit, which the woman then gathers."

MELVILLE ISLAND   Among the Tiwi people of Melville Island, a girl achieves special status with her first blood: she is called "Murinaleta" for four menstrual periods. During her first menstrual period the Murinaleta leaves the general community and goes out into the wild with other women to set up a new camp. She is usually accompanied by her mother, her co-wives (she is already married) and any other older women. No men are allowed in the camp. During this time she is not allowed to touch water, or even a container holding water, so other women hold water to her lips. She is also not allowed to look at any bodies of water, because spirit beings in the water may kill her if she does. There are many taboos to follow the first time beside these, she also is not allowed to speak, or scratch her own skin. After this first special time she, like all other women, will have less strict precautions to take during her periods.

JAPAN   This just a little observation: in Japan today tampons come with little plastic finger coverings - like cut-off fingers of gloves - so that women do not have to touch themselves "down there" when they put in a tampon. This might sound a bit weird, but tampons which come with applicators like the popular brands used by women in England and the United States seem strange to European women whose tampons usually come without applicators. We have applicators so, like the Japanese women, we do not have to touch ourselves "down there"!

AUSTRALIA   Aboriginal Australian men exercise ritual power through ceremonies in which they cut themselves to imitate women's menstruation. In some tribes men actually cut open their penises to reproduce the look of a bleeding vulva. They say that the women used to perform these ceremonies, that all of this ritual power really belongs to women (though their blood), but that men have learned how to trick women:
"But really we have been stealing what belongs to them (the women), for it is mostly all women's business; and since it concerns them it belongs to them. Men have nothing to do really, except copulate, it belongs to the women, All that belonging to those Wuwalak (legendary bleeding sisters), the baby, the blood, the yelling, their dancing, all that concerns the women; but every time we have to trick them. Women can't see what men are doing, although it really is their own business, but we can see their side... In the beginning we had nothing, because men had been doing nothing; we took these things from women."

48

Aboriginal Australian women make a cat's cradle design called "the menstrual blood of three women". They usually make this design when there are only women around. If a man walks past he will not look at their game because it is part of the domain of women. Cat's cradles such as this may be used in their rituals for a girl's first menstruation.

Native Tribes Of North America:

The Hopi   The Hopi, like many other peoples, have myths about the magical powers of menstrual blood. "The Bloody Maiden Who Looks After Animals" is a mythological woman, who, legend has it, was angry at some Hopi hunters. She killed them, and then appeared before all of the people covered with blood. She grabbed a live antelope with one hand, and wiped her other hand over her vulva. She wiped this hand on the antelope's nose, and twisted its nose, and then let it free. She then told the people that from then on it would be very hard for them to hunt the antelope.

The Navaho   The Navahos have a ceremony for menarche called Kinaaldá, which continues today. It is considered the most important of their religious rites. Its purpose is to teach that menstruation and sex are holy and fruitful. The menstruating girl is secluded and given instruction by the women of the tribe, and afterward there is a great celebration in which the entire community is involved. Girls may go through more this ceremony more than once during their first year of menstruation.

The Yurok   An anthropologist was visiting the home of a friend of his who was a member of the Yurok tribe of Northern California On the way home, his friend explained to the anthropologist that his wife was having her period, and so would not be joining them for dinner. The anthropologist was surprised that his friend and his wife followed the old ways of isolating women during their period. When they got to the house the wife appeared and explained that while she didn't have a menstrual hut to go to, she often stayed in the back room of their house during her period. Sometimes, though, she became restless and came out to talk, like tonight. The anthropologist asked her why she followed the old ways, and she explained that when she was very young, she was raised in non-Indian foster homes, where she was taught that menstruation was shameful, a punishment for women. When she returned to Yurok society her aunts and her grandmother, who were very well respected women, taught her differently, they trained her in the Yurok menstrual rules.

These rules say that when a woman is menstruating she is very powerful, and she should isolate herself at this time so that she should not waste her energy on every day matters, or have her concentration broken by members of the opposite sex.

She learned that all of her energy should go toward meditating on the purpose of her life, and the gathering of her spiritual energy. The menstrual shelter is the equivalent of the men's sweathouse, a place where you go to look into yourself and make yourself stronger. They believe the flow of blood helps purify a woman's body for spiritual tasks.

Through practicing the menstrual traditions women come to see that "the earth has her own moontime" and understanding that makes women stronger and proud of their own cycle. The Yurok woman also said that in the old days all of the village women who were fertile had their periods at the same time, so all of them would leave to go to the menstrual shelter at once. The men of the village used that time to go and train in their own traditions in their sweathouse.

disclaimers: Most of this information was found in books by anthropologists, people who go live with and study other people. Some of this might be outdated. People who didn't have much contact with the industrialized world can quickly become part of our "global village" and take on Western/Christian attitudes and leave their traditional ways behind.

Image: Young Women enjoy celebrating their Menarche

Menstrual Tips from Real Women! (what tips would you share?)

Use your pre-menstrual energy to clean the house and prepare food so you can relax and not have to take care of others while you are bleeding.	Wear red. It stimulates the circulation and replaces the red you are losing from the aura.	H o o o w l at the moon
To avoid cramping and menstrual pain, try not eating or drinking cold foods and drinks during and up to 5 days before your period.	One thing that helps a lot to relieve menstrual tension is a really good back massage, especially focusing on the pressure points and tender spots between the lower shoulder blades and the spine. A flexible woman can do this herself fairly well. It is easier with a friend though. Massage should be deep and slow, with a lot of pressure but not so much that it hurts.	Spend time by the ocean. Use the beauty and power of nature, especially water, to cleanse, clarify and wash away the old and no longer useful thoughts and feelings. Long, hot, perfumed soaks in the bath are great. Clary Sage and Rose oils are lovely.
Often, our rage at this time can be seen as a way of driving people away, so make sure you spend time alone. Use this energy to clear up unfinished relationship difficulties.		Screaming in a secluded place- a beach or hill or forest is highly recommended.
Celebrate your womanhood	All things grow with water. Release your tears and fear not the murky depths of your unconscious. Use your menstrual time to bring the mind home and contact your true nature.	Take care of your diet and try to avoid fatty foods and processed foods, coffee, tea, fizzy drinks etc in the second half of your cycle.

Avoid dairy products!

For sore breasts, massage in circular movements, up, in, down and around the breasts. Also try using a crystallized salt deodorant instead of conventional ones.

Be selective about how and who you spend your time with !

Evening Primrose Oil (HIGH doses) and St John's Wort oil capsules have helped me immensely. Lessens the severe cramping I was getting as well as the depression and rage. I'm not nearly as psychotic as I used to be, period or not :-)

Try switching from paper pads and tampons to cloth pads.

I try to take a moon lodge day sometime during my flow, preferably the first day. i find that tarot reading is especially insightful during my moon time also. I take vitex extract regularly and it has eased my heavy flow. also, raspberry leaf tea is wonderful, there are plenty of women's menstrual teas available There are lots of books that are excellent resources with things like suggestions for honouring your flow such as creating a blood jar from your (cloth) pads and using the blood water to nourish your houseplants.

Judy Grahn in an article entitled "From Sacred Blood to the Curse and Beyond," argues that it was the ability to add our blood to the seed that first "fertilized" the grain and domesticated it. (She rests the whole of women's original claim on spirituality upon our sacred blood, our being "She who bleeds but does not die." An interesting article!) Our culture is programmed with disgust at women's blood. One way of maintaining that disgust is to require "sanitary" napkins filled with chemicals that take blood and turn it into something with a nauseating smell and look.

Zinc relieves cramps--eat dark green veggies like spinach!--and potassium relieves bloating, so eat those bananas too. Both need to be eaten in the second half of your cycle. Works for me!

Laugh with your best girlfriend.

To all of you who have an especially rough time with your periods, my own change in attitude about my body and its moon cycles have made a tremendous difference in my life. blessed be!

Drink hot red teas, especially no caffeine herb teas, like Cranberry Apple, Blackcurrant and Raspberry Leaf. Savour the colourful flow as it spreads into the water, while it steeps

Using cloth reminds us that blood does not smell bad, nor look disgusting. Using pretty, soft cloth affirms our willingness to touch and address our blood with honour. It also is more respectful of Mother Gaia not to fill her with destructive chemical, plastic and paper substances, but to return what we receive with care.

Have a day off.
~~~
I've found this to be my best medicine. Meditate, dance wildly, be creative, watch the moon, sleep more, read, do nothing, do whatever turns you on.

Flaxseed oil every day. Natural progesterone (from yams) eliminated my menstrual migraines. What a relief!


~~~

At night, nothing beats my old hot-water bottle! Wrap a towel around it and put over the cramp... Mmmmm....!

One time I had horribly bad cramps. Luckily, my boyfriend was there for me. He filled the tub up with hot water and put some nicely scented bath salts in and I sat in there and relaxed. After about 20-30 minutes, my cramps were better! Try it :) –

Gather a group of women together, the more diverse the group the better. Tell them in advance that you'll be getting together to talk about your moon time. Have everyone bring food. Make herbal tea. Share stories about your menses and what it has meant to you. It's so empowering to be able to share these stories with other women

Eat lots of chocolate, drink lots of herbal tea. Stay in bed for a week, watch soap operas on TV. You don't have to pretend you feel fine when you don't. Just do whatever makes you happy!!

Since menstruation is a time of release, use it to free yourself from the things that bind you, literally as well as figuratively. Wear your hair down. Take off your rings, and, in the house, most of your clothes. Exercise only if you love it, not because of the calories burned. Don't volunteer for anything out of a sense of duty. Get a massage. In short, think of yourself first for a while, and at the end of your cycle, you can pick up your burdens relaxed and refreshed.

I get severe cramps, like so severe that untreated I would be vomiting, passing out, crying and unable to walk for up to 5 days. Things that help me are: a lot of massage, hot water bottles, herbal remedies such as Dong Quai, fish oil and evening primrose oil, and dietary changes such as Absolutely no salt, sugar, caffeine, alcohol, etc. I exercise every day except the ones where my cramps are severe. I still have 1 day of cramps!

A tip on working with cramps: I have had bad cramps for years and have shifted in the way I work with them. I used to totally disconnect from my bleeding by taking strong painkillers & using tampons. I now do neither. I use Moon Times Cloth Pads (which are wonderful) & instead of shutting down the pain I am learning to allow myself to feel it to the fullest extent. When I allow myself to embrace this fear of pain & merge with it, it changes. I place my hands one on top of the other over my womb area & breathe gently in the nose & out through the mouth. I listen to my body. Sometimes I cry or howl whilst doing this and at times it feels as if the pain is not mine alone. I cry as I allow myself to feel the pain of a global community of women, who I am connected to through my bleeding. I cry tears for those who will not give themselves the space to feel. "You can't heal it until you feel it" a friend once said to me. It's true. My cramps are much less now & I actually don't mind them. They remind me to take time out to feel, breathe & connect with the wisdom of my body.

Exercise is great for me, but not only during my bleeding.. Also, I'm a veggie so my cramps aren't so bad. Even if you aren't veggie, I strongly suggest not eating meat of any sort for about four days before, and right through your bleeding. I find also that I'm absolutely neurotic for about two days at the beginning, so I find it useful to look back on the month and wonder at the shift in consciousness when it's all over. Try it.

For several years, I have practiced the spiritual discipline of isolating- going within during my menstrual cycle, to pray for vision and my Relatives and to honour my body by giving it time for rest and renewal. This is by far the most powerful single thing I've ever done to create a positive and beautiful experience where there once was pain, irritation and discomfort. Part of my spiritual work this time around involves letting women know about this wonderful tool for balance, wellness and spiritual strength.

Also, I take a fabulous Women's Formula (I make my own) Tincture out of Red Raspberry, Cramp Bark, Squaw Vine, Catnip and Black Cohosh. Terrific for cramps, relaxing and even good for muscles spasms elsewhere (like sore neck and shoulder muscles from too much computer work!)

Tips for cramps: flannel pyjamas and a hot water bottle are a must. The best remedy I have found for when I can't stay in bed with the above items is cramp bark tincture. I can actually still feel my uterus contracting but it doesn't hurt! Combine all this with love & insight into your cramps.

I made myself a menstrual colouring book from images in books that were powerful to me- copied them onto heavy watercolour type paper at the local copy shop and punched holes in the edges and bound with red ribbon. Every month when I am on my heaviest bleeding day, I light candles and sit in front of my altar, meditate, take time for me, and paint in my colouring book with my menstrual blood. After the blood is collected, I use a special brush that is for nothing else, and paint a sacred picture in my colouring book, sometimes two or three depending on how inspired I am. I make them into spells by adding words and my intentions.

A friend of mine told me that she read somewhere that there are four phases associated with the four days of bleeding- First day is Reflection (looking back on the month), second day is Projection (your plans for the month ahead), third day is Purification (the heaviest blood has usually passed by now and it is time for cleansing), fourth day is Celebration (need I say more?) Thought this was a nice way to be with your cycle. Enjoy!

A Red Tent

This beautiful red tent was in the healing field at Glastonbury Festival 2003. It was just there as a retreat space for women to go to. I tried to find out who had created it- but sadly never did.

Moon Time Foods:

Red Moon Juice

use a juicer!
4 carrots
1 beetroot
1 apple
a slice of ginger
YUM!

Raspberry Smoothie

1 cup or raspberries (frozen or fresh), ½ cup of yogurt
1 cup of hibiscus tea
a pinch of cinnamon and cardamom

Beetroot soup

4 chopped beetroots
4 stick of celery- chopped
3 carrots- chopped
1 leek- chopped
1 onion- chopped
2 cloves of garlic- chopped
herbs; mixed, or thyme, parley, rosemary
1 bay leaf
2 tablespoons of dandelion leaf
add salt & pepper to taste

sauté the onions and garlic with herbs (not the dandelion leaf) in a little olive oil,
add some water and the carrots, celery, leeks, beetroot, simmer and blend as
required- garnish with the dandelion leaf.

Take a Sacred Day Each Month

I see PMT as a modern day disease/dis-ease. In cultures where women are more in tune with nature and their cycles, where they eat 'real' (natural) foods, where they work hard but not in offices, not in front of computer screens all day- PMT doesn't exist!

So if we break it down in to simple steps perhaps we too can eradicate PMT!

Your Sacred Day…the first thing I strongly suggest is keeping your first bleeding day as SACRED! This is the time to retreat, ignore the outer world, switch off your phones, facebook, the TV, the radio, and instead go within yourself, ask yourself what you need. This is your time to GET CLEAR, RELEASE and LET GO of whats not needed in your life!

On the first day of your moontime your intuition is higher than ANY OTHER day of the month!

When we take this time out to go within, we tune in to our inner power, which then releases dreams and ideas for us to use later in the month.

After nurturing ourselves in this way we will feel replenished and feel as if we have a fresh start; a chance to begin again. We are so lucky to have this chance to rebirth EVERY MONTH! WHAT A BLESSING!

If every woman started to take this time out we will CREATE CHANGE IN THE WORLD! So you may have to be 'selfish' to make this happen for yourself. Be clear that this is a day to REST and SELF NOURISH. You are being selfish now so you can be selfless later in the month!

At this time you are sensitive and vulnerable, you need this sacred day to protect yourself. *Even if you only have 5 mins before you get out of bed, do something that nurtures you and helps you develop an inner attitude of rest and renewal for the rest of the day.*

Some ideas of what you can do: journalling, meditation, silence (go within and allow your insight to come though the silence), yoga, movement, tai chi, chi gong.

Take this time to allow your body to detox and purify, by eating nourishing foods; root vegetables are grounding, leafy greens are detoxing, eat healthy fats-coconut, avocado, seeds and nuts.

Drink water and gentle herb teas such as raspberry leaf. (raspberry leaf gives strength and is beneficial even to menopausal, non bleeding women)

Avoid toxifying foods; processed foods, alcohol, caffeine, fatty fried foods.

Keep your diet simple to support your body to cleanse itself.

How Do We "Go Within?"

Most of us live have very busy lives and find it hard to say no to things to allow us some 'me time' and quite space.

There are so many "shoulds" planning our daily schedule. So be courageous, say "No" to the things you don't want to do, ask your family for support and take some time for yourself.

This means turning off your TV and computer (now that's courageous!) and tuning into yourself. So much in life distracts our energy and stops us from searching for deeper truth and meaning.

Consider the impact of focusing our energies only on activities that enliven our search for deeper meaning. Taking time out helps deepen into a search for our true calling: that which finds its source in inspiration, gifting and joyfulness. Think of your life and your activities; use this quiet time to reconsider how to be generous with your time and love, while figuring out a way to fill your life with work and activities that feed your spirit.

Another thing you could focus on is to look at what you dislike outside of yourself, and then look within to find where it lives within you. That is your shadow, the projection onto external reality of the darkness that lives within you. Remind yourself that you have the power to find your own truth, by looking inward with a truthful eye.

Meaning doesn't live somewhere far away. It is not in heaven, it is not in the words of some 'spiritual person', it is not in church, it is not in school, it is not in your government, it is not in your guides or angel.....

The Earth is speaking to you, every minute of every day! The answers you seek are in the wind, the movement of the waves, in the activity in a bee hive or an ant hill, in the intelligence that moves the stars and planets, in the storms and earthquakes, in the songs of birds, in the howl of a wolf, in the grace of a deer, in the smile of your parent/friend, in the flowing water of a river, in the shape of a cloud, in the cosmic music of the shimmering particles and waves that make up our universe!

Go outside, be in nature and tune in to the teachings of Mother Earth, listen deeply to the existent wisdom of our world. Accepting the animal part of humanity as a source of knowledge will help bring harmony, peace and generosity back to lives.

It is time to initiate a new quest for spiritual knowledge. Take stock and question your current beliefs, whatever they may be. Be open. Seek knowledge from cultures and spiritual traditions that exist all around the globe. Don't concentrate solely on seeking an intellectual understanding of spirituality through written or spoken words. If you haven't tried to do a ritual yet, this is the time to start. Just open up and listen, you will know exactly what to do!

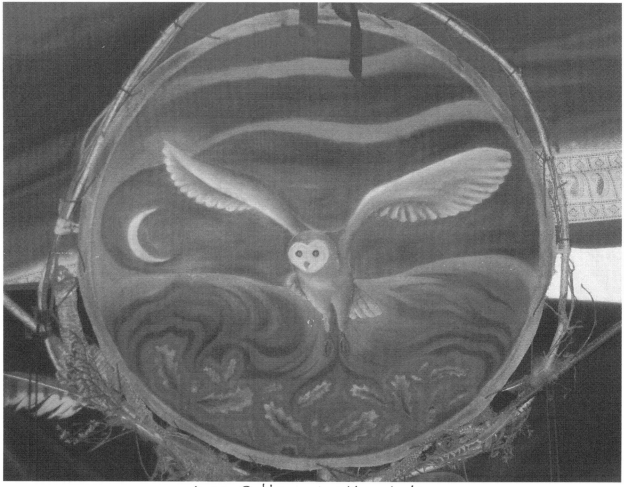

Image: Owl banner in a Moon Lodge

Dear Mother Moon ... 'write in' section featuring your questions about your cycle and other 'Moon Time' related things....

Dear Mother Moon, I am really interested in using cloth pads- having considered making my own in the past but not being sure how to make them absorbent enough. I have a really heavy flow and flood a lot. Are cloth pads absorbent enough to cope with this? Many thanks, Lyds

Hi Lyds, My daughter has suffered with menorrhagia (very heavy periods) and found cloth pads more absorbent than the super night time pads- and she said she wasn't scared of leaking or flooding in them! (Her bleeding isn't so bad now after using a 'Liver Tonic' drink recommended by her naturopath)

Also you may find your bleeding lessens when using a more natural sanitary protection.

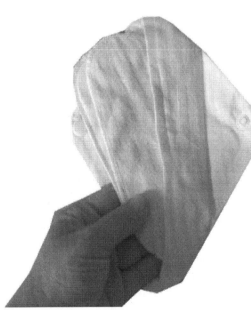

The design of the Moon Times Pads, with the wings and choice of different inserts are extremely efficient. If you choose the right amount of inserts for the absorbency of your flow, the pads should not leak at all.

For extra security there are inserts made from a double layer of towelling with a polyurethane backing!

Image- showing inserts being put in to a pad

Not using enough inserts is usually the cause of leaking, so use more inserts; 1 or 2 is suitable for light to med flow, 2 -4 for medium to heavy. Towelling inserts are the most absorbent!

Good luck & bright blessings, Mother Moon xxxx

Dear Mother Moon, Do you know how long it's OK to leave a Mooncup in and are there risks with Toxic Shock Syndrome? Katherine, Bristol.

Hi Katherine, I checked out with Mooncup about how long its ok to leave them

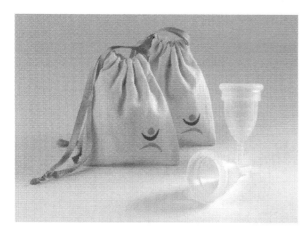

in- they recommend changing it at least every 6 hours. Although they say there is no link between TSS and Mooncups- I would still be wary! Personally I don't think it's a good idea to put *anything* (well almost anything!!) in your vagina! I occasionally use a sponge but try to avoid it if I can.

Image: Mooncup

I know women who prefer not to use disposables find Mooncups and sponges easier for the work environment or for travelling than washable pads (my preference) - my only answer to that is try not to work or travel when on your Moon! I know I'm really lucky to be self employed- so I can adjust my work load and avoid work altogether when I'm bleeding, I would still recommend taking things easy when bleeding, allow yourself the time to bleed and dream.

Some info on TSS: Research has determined that there are health risks associated with conventional tampon usage. These risks are related to the use of Dioxin, a by-product of the tampon fibre's bleaching process. Risk associated to Dioxin exposure and synthetic fibres are: endometriosis, ovarian, cervical and breast cancers, immune system deficiencies, pelvic inflammatory diseases, reduced fertility and Toxic Shock Syndrome (TSS). Toxic Shock Syndrome develops when the common bacteria, Staphylococcus aureus, produce a toxin which is absorbed into the bloodstream. The toxin rapidly overwhelms the immune system and attacks the major organs, leading to kidney failure, collapse of the lungs and in severe cases, cardiac arrest.

Alarmingly, half of all known cases of Toxic Shock are women using Tampons. *Inserting anything slightly abrasive in to the vagina can cause tiny cuts and imbed pieces into the delicate tissue of the vaginal walls. This has been traced as the probable cause of Toxic Shock Syndrome and has been shown to damage the vaginal walls by causing ulceration and peeling of the mucous membrane.*

Although TSS is most common in women using tampons, it can occur in children, infants and men as a result of infection with Staphylococcus aureus. About half of all cases are the result of infection associated with tampon use with the remaining cases due to other localised infections, for example skin or wound infections following burns, insect bites or surgery. The risk of TSS is greater in younger people because older people are more likely to have developed the necessary antibodies to protect them. Tampons soak up more than just blood, they also absorb vaginal mucus that is necessary to maintain a healthy pH balance in the vagina. The vaginal walls are the most absorbent part of a woman's body. Twenty five per cent of all pesticides are used on all cotton, which are used to make tampons

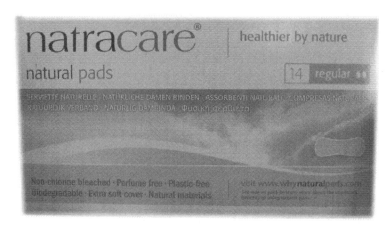

Some other alternatives in sanitary protection...
Have you thought about using washable sanitary protection at night instead of a Mooncup- such as cloth pads or natural sponges? Some of the 'disposables' are more eco-friendly than others. If you don't fancy washables then switch to organic cotton pads- Natracare make these and they are available in most health shops and some supermarkets. These organic pads don't have the harmful chemicals and are made from non GM cotton. They are also safe to put in your compost bin!

Much love Mother Moon x

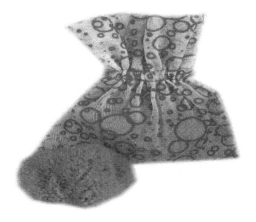

Images: top;pack of Natracare pads, centre; Moon Times Cloth Pads, bottom;unbleached Natural Menstrual Sponge Tampon

Dear Mother Moon, I've been suffering from Irritable Bowel Syndrome- IBS- for a year or so- I've tried loads of different things- changing my diet, herbal remedies, de-stressing techniques etc.
Recently my doctor mentioned that IBS can be a pre-menstrual symptom and she suggested I note when my IBS is worse- and the outcome the last 2 months has been that it flares up pre-menstrually! I wondered if you have any tips for alleviating this? Are there any herbal remedies? Thank you , Star

Hi Star, IBS is mostly caused by stress- so it would make sense that women can suffer with IBS pre-menstrually.

I would treat IBS similarly to PMT. Firstly plenty of rest and relaxation – make some time for yourself, time to just 'be'. Create your own 'moon lodge', a quiet space to meditate in, do yoga, write, dream, draw, sew or make things.

Eating a healthy balanced diet is important. Try to avoid foods like coffee, tea, alcohol, sugar and anything containing sugar, artificial flavourings and colourings, processed foods, wheat and wheat products, meat, cigarettes, drugs, chocolate, fizzy caffeinated drinks, milk and milk products- *basically all the refined and junk foods in the pre menstrual phase.*

Eat lots of fresh fruit and vegetables and healthy stuff that allows your body to detoxify for awhile. It's only for a few days- try it and notice the difference! By giving our bodies the nutrients it needs (essential for a healthy body and healthy cycle!) our PMT becomes more manageable and as our body is supported and nurtured our body will support us on the other levels- mental, emotional, and spiritual.
Herbal teas are great- either see a herbalist or look in health food shops for ready made menstrual mixes. Certain vitamins and minerals can be useful.
Aromatherapy products can work really well.
Exercise is another important factor - try going for a run or a bit of yoga- you won't feel like doing it- but it will be worth a try! And don't forget orgasms are a great way to release tension from the pelvic area!

Our relationship to our reproductive organs or female parts is a reflection of our own ease or dis-ease with our feminine expression in the world. As you heal and address your relationship with your cycle your IBS PMT will decrease.

Good luck and best wishes, Mother Moon xxxx

Dear Mother Moon , What exactly is a Moon Lodge? Could you explain? Thanks Kate.

Hi Kate, well, The Moon lodge originates from the Native American Indian tradition. They honoured the moon time as sacred, it was treated with respect.

The Moon Lodge is a Sacred Place for women to gather during their Bleeding Time. It was when we connected to Moon and Earth, Grandmother and Mother, and to each other.

We were welcomed back into our communities, which eagerly awaited our return, to hear the wisdom we had gained.

Image- Moon Lodge Tipi

In these modern, changing times, women are reconnecting with and recreating the Moon Lodge Ceremonies. We are discovering our voices and our inherent role as Wisdom Keepers.

. Among our dreaming peoples, the most prophetic dreams and visions were brought to the people through the Moon Lodge. In other words, the most useful information that can come to us comes from each of you women who use your moon time well.

For each of us who do not honour this time, much is lost, including the respect of others for our bleeding.

At the first Red Web Conference that their fantasy was that there would be a Moon Lodge in every town and that there would be some type of directory so one could just look it up and then drop in. What an amazing thought!

Setting up monthly Full Moon gatherings are a step towards building a local community a Moon Lodge- but for me the Lodge isn't an actual space- it is the women who take part.

Much love & blessings, Mother Moon xxxx

Dear Mother Moon, my daughter has had her moon time for a year or so now, but experiences such pain she vomits. Do you have any suggestions to help her ease this? Thanks for all your wisdom – Lou.

Dear Lou, I am so sorry to hear about your daughter, what an awful experience of her moontime.

Firstly lets address the pain issue- in Chinese medicine pain is usually a sign of stagnation and it is that which is causing rebellious stomach chi. A woman's normal cycle is one spent making blood in the month and then loosing blood. So anything that disrupts that cycle can cause problems.

What is her diet like? If the body hasn't got enough good quality blood- menstruation can be very challenging. Also other things that can cause stagnation are emotions and stress. Sugar and caffeine can wreak havoc with a menstruation cycle.

Shiatsu, acupuncture, flower essences and homeopathy which all address the emotional side of things should help things flow a bit easier by balancing both hormones & feelings.

Dehydration can cause period pain, drinking extra fluids in the 2-3 days before your moontime helps enormously.

Warm bath in epsom salt or mix 1tsp epsom salt in warm water and drink slowly, or take magnesium, hot water bottle, vitamin c, lemon and honey tea, finding ways to de-stress.

She could also try the pelvic rock exercise (google pelvic rock exercise or see this link) http://www.hala-hi.org/wp-content/uploads/2012/06/Pelvic-Tilt-as-first-aid-for-Dysmenorrhoea.png

A high dose (500mg daily) calcium & magnesium supplement (ideally taken pre-menses but start now) hot baths or compress on the womb area with chamomile tea and lavender essential oil. Pulsatilla 30c . Raspberry leaf, Mugwort, Yarrow, Valerian, Black Cohosh, Cramp Bark – in whatever form you can find from health food shop.

Seeing a homeopath may help- they will discuss diet and other aspects of her life. So much going on for young people. Tampons, parabens, junk/processed foods, dehydration and stress impact on health especially fertility health.

She could also wear a little magnet called MN8 a day before and during moon time (search it on Amazon)

Castor oil packs (between bleeds, not during her period) see You Tube for videos 'how to make a castor oil pack' or my You Tube Channel http://www.youtube.com/MoonTimesPads Maya abdominal massage works wonders too. (see You Tube again!)

I hope all of this helps, Love Mother Moon xxx

Dear Mother Moon,
My daughter is 12 and has had her period for about a year. She is suffering from very heavy periods and our GP wants to try her on the Pill which I am totally against ....do you have any suggestions? Ruth, Merseyside

Hi Ruth, My daughter suffered from heavy periods too! A herbalist suggested a liver cleanse drink- which I did with her, It normalised her periods and we both felt really healthy- our skin glowed and we had more energy too! It tastes a bit like salad dressing though! I added more apple juice than the recipe in this book to make it taste better! Other than the drink, you may want to check the suggestions in the previous query.

Good Luck, love, Mother Moon xxx

Phases of the Moon

Menarche Work in Primary Schools (written 2005)

Imagine a school that embraced Celebrating Menarche- a school that invited mothers of young girls to come and talk openly about the changes women face in puberty, to honour their daughters rite of passage and explore their own journey with their moon flow, a school that promoted eco sanitary wear and allowed their students to wear their moon necklaces with pride! This has been a vision of mine for many years and the vision has begun to manifest! In 2005 I was invited to run a Celebrating Menarche Workshop at a local primary school! Initially the idea was for me to come to school and talk to the young women about menstruation, sanitary wear and celebrating their menarche- but I had other ideas! I insisted that the mothers be involved- after all, what is the point of honouring a girl's menstruation if she was going home to a family that held it as taboo? I knew that for girls to truly honour their cycle they need the support of their mothers, and of course many mothers don't know the secrets our bleeding time holds- so I had to be able to address these issues; support the mothers to support their daughters!I discussed this with the school and they agreed, deciding it would be best to tie the workshop in with their sex education classes. So we planned to run the workshop one evening in November. Five mothers and their daughters arrived at the school and were amazed at the transformation of one of the class rooms- we had moved back the tables and chairs, I cleared the energies of the room using Reiki symbols, scattered the floor with furry beanbags and soft red velvet cushions. I created an altar in the middle; spreading a red glittery cloth on the floor, lighting candles and incense, adding my goddess figures, some crystals, shells, precious beads and stones, flowers, pictures, water collected from all the ceremonies and altars I have made and lastly I sprinkled it with chocolate and glitter! The atmosphere was completely changed!Playing in the background was my "women's workshops" CD- a mix of inspirational female musicians- from Peru to Sinead O'Connor, Madonna to Carolyn Hillyer, and so the evening began.

Initially I could sense the apprehension from both the girls and their mothers- for some of them they were stepping in to a mystery they had no comprehension of, but they were courageous and willing and I honoured them for that. We began with a reading of quotes I had gathered from books and women I have met- describing their menarche, we each took a turn to speak a little about ourselves (I learned that the ages ranged from 7-10 years old and one of the mothers shared that she was menstruating that evening!) and went over the ground rules for the group.

The rest of the evening was spent sharing some chamomile and rose tea, listening to a menarche story, having hand massages, discussions, making moon necklaces (one to represent our bleeding time and one for ovulation), we looked at choices in sanitary products and had an opportunity to browse my collection of 'Menstruation Literature' that travels with me from women's group to women's group, moon lodge to moon lodge! The evening flew by and everyone wished for more time, remarks from mums and daughters were "what gentleness", "a great idea for girls and women!" "It was better that we expected- we really enjoyed it" "Reminded me my cycle is something to celebrate" "a wonderful chance to be close and focus on our relationship", "my daughter was very apprehensive but soon relaxed", "I liked the shrine, the sweets, tea, bead making, massage, being in a circle, the massage oil and the incense!" "Thank you very very much" "how do we get more women doing this?" The evening felt like an enormous break through for my menarche work- and I trust that this ripple will spread .....to goddess knows where!

Image; Mums and Daughters attending the 'Journey into Menarche' Workshop in a Bristol School.

What girls told me about 'why its great to be a girl'...

We get to eat lost of chocolate!
We are creative
We have fun dressing up
We have more choices than boys- we can do ANYTHING!
We are neat, organised and we don't mess around as much as boys!
We love to chat!
We feel good when we hang out with other girls.
We laugh a lot!
We have so much choice in what to wear.
We get to have changeable moods
We can have babies and make milk.
Our bodies are amazing!
We can wear bright colours, make up, jewellry, high heels, hair accessories.
We don't fight when we get angry
We cry and let our stresses out.
We talk things over with our girl friends
We are tough!
We ROCK!
We are smart :)
We can wear pink and not be embarrassed!
We talk about our feelings.
We get nice toilets.
We aren't violent

WE LOVE BEING GIRLS!

What things would you and your friends add to the list?

....

....

....

....

....

Recommended Books

The Seven Sacred Rites of Menarche: The Spiritual Journey of the Adolescent Girl by Kristi Meisenbach Boylan
The vast majority of books on menarche-the first menstrual cycle-do not address its effect on a young girl's spiritual journey from maidenhood to womanhood. This book outlines the seven rituals, or stepping-stones, that a young woman faces on her voyage, marking her way through adolescence. These stepping-stones lead her from the childhood years to the childbearing years and draw attention to a young woman's changing spirit. Included are ideas for creating rites of passage, celebrations, and positive rituals for both mothers and daughters to share during this challenging and amazing time of growth

Daughters of the Moon, Sisters of the Sun: Young Women and Mentors on the Transition to Womanhood by K. Wind Hughes,
Twenty-one young women share life lessons, coming-of-age stories, and interviews with the remarkable women who influenced their growth

A Toolbox for Our Daughters: Building Strength, Confidence and Integrity by Annette Geffert, Diane Brown
Sensible real life strategies to build a girls self esteem. It provides useful exercises for helping girls grow in their relationships with others, with their own inner lives and with our endangered world.

Celebrating Girls: Nurturing and Empowering Our Daughters by Virginia Beane Rutter
As girls grow up they may face many different dilemmas such as pregnancy at a young age or loss of self-esteem. This book offers practical tips to parents and other carers on how to support girls from infancy to adolescence, each chapter focusing on a different stage in a girl's development.

Say What You Mean, Get What You Want by Tricia Kreitman,
Explaining to young people how to make a stand and assert themselves, this advice book deals with how to judge and evaluate situations and relationships, and how to develop negotiating skills. Each chapter is illustrated and explained with letters and accounts from real teenagers.

Soul Searching-A girls guide to finding herself by Sarah Stillman
Written by a 16yr old girl- she gives advice for discovering what is really important in life, covering topics such as managing stress, finding inner peace, exploring dreams, and cultivating a meaningful life.

Have You Started Yet? Getting the Facts Straight by Ruth Thompson.
Starting to have periods is something all girls face. This book explains exactly what periods are, why they happen, and how they will affect you; asking all the questions and giving all the answers simply and openly, with plenty of practical advice

Wild Girls: The Path of the Young Goddess by Patricia Monaghan
Maiden, mother, crone; of the three faces of the goddess, the maiden corresponds to the part of a woman's soul that is always questing, exploring, and free to move. The stories in this book represent some of the many visions of the "Wild Girl" throughout the world, each is followed by commentary and activities, such as building an altar, creating healing rituals, and working with dreams

Don't Give It Away! by Iyanla Vanzant
A workbook in which teenage girls can explore their thoughts and feelings about the things most important to them: family, friends, body image and love life.

Power Thoughts for Teens by Louise L. Hay
Louise Hay has assisted many people in discovering and using the full potential of their own creative powers for personal growth and self-healing. She contends that affirmations are powerful tools and encourages people to use them to expedite their personal growth process.

The Red Tent by Anita Diamant
This book is a firm favourite of mine and is an epic celebration of womanhood, written for women everywhere, regardless of their status, creed or colour. It is the story of a woman whose life was blessed by great love and torn by tragedy, of the lessons she learned through her own experiences and those of the women, and men, whose lives she touched. The red tent is the place where women gathered during their cycles of birthing, menses and even illness.

Mother-Daughter Wisdom: Understanding the Crucial Link Between Mothers, Daughters, and Health by Dr Christiane Northrup
With such groundbreaking bestsellers as Women's Bodies, Women's Wisdom and The Wisdom of Menopause, Dr. Christiane Northrup is one of today's most trusted and visionary medical experts. Now she presents her most profound and revolutionary approach to women's health. . . .
The mother-daughter relationship sets the stage for our state of health and well-being for our entire lives. Because our mothers are our first and most powerful female role models, our most deeply ingrained beliefs about ourselves as women

come from them. And our behaviour in relationships—with food, with our children, with our mates, and with ourselves—is a reflection of those beliefs. Once we understand our mother-daughter bonds, we can rebuild our own health, whatever our age, and create a lasting positive legacy for the next generation. Mother-Daughter Wisdom introduces an entirely new map of female development, exploring the "five facets of feminine power," which range from the basics of physical self-care to the discovery of passion and purpose in life. This blueprint allows any woman—whether or not she has children—to repair the gaps in her own upbringing and create a better adult relationship with her mother. If she has her own daughter, it will help her be the mother she has always wanted to be.

Drawing on patient case histories and personal experiences, Dr. Northrup also presents findings at the cutting edge of medicine and psychology. Discover:

⬦How to lay the nutritional foundation to prevent eating disorders and adult diseases

⬦The truth about the immunization controversy–and the true meaning of immunity

⬦How we can change our genetic health legacy

⬦Why financial literacy is essential to women's health

⬦How to foster healthy sexuality and future "love maps" in our daughters

⬦How to balance independence with caring, and individual growth with family ties

Written with warmth, enthusiasm, and rare intelligence, Mother-Daughter Wisdom is an indispensable book destined to change lives and become essential reading for all women.

Beautiful Girl: Celebrating the Wonders of Your Body by Dr. Christiane Northrup

For years Christiane Northrup, MD, has taught women about heath, wellness and the miracle of their bodies. Now, in her first children's book, she presents these ideas to the youngest of girls. Beautiful Girl presents this simple but important message: that to be born female is a very special thing and carries with it magical gifts and powers that must be recognized and nurtured. Dr Northrup believes that helping girls learn at a young age to value the wonder and uniqueness of their bodies can have positive benefits that will last throughout their lives. By reading this lovely book, little girls will learn how their bodies are perfect just the way they are, the importance of treating themselves with gentle care, and how changes are just a part of growing up.

Steve Biddulph's Raising Girls by Steve Biddulph

Steve Biddulph's Raising Boys was a global phenomenon. The first book in a generation to look at boys' specific needs, parents loved its clarity and warm insights into their sons' inner world. But today, things have changed. It's girls that are in trouble.

There has been a sudden and universal deterioration in girls' mental health, starting in primary school and devastating the teen years.

Steve Biddulph's Raising Girls is both a guidebook and a call-to-arms for parents. The five key stages of girlhood are laid out so that you know exactly what matters at which age, and how to build strength and connectedness into your daughter from infancy onwards. Raising Girls is both fierce and tender in its mission to help girls more at every age. It's a book for parents who love their daughters deeply, whether they are newborns, teenagers, young women – or anywhere in between. Feeling secure, becoming an explorer, getting along with others, finding her soul, and becoming a woman – at last, there is a clear map of girls' minds that accepts no limitations, narrow roles or selling-out of your daughter's potential or uniqueness.

All the hazards are signposted – bullying, eating disorders, body image and depression, social media harms and helps – as are concrete and simple measures for both mums and dads to help prevent their daughters from becoming victims. Parenthood is restored to an exciting journey, not one worry after another, as it's so often portrayed.

Steve talks to the world's leading voices on girls' needs and makes their ideas clear and simple, adding his own humour and experience through stories that you will never forget. Even the illustrations, by Kimio Kubo, provide unique and moving glimpses into the inner lives of girls.

Along with his fellow psychologists worldwide, Steve is angry at the exploitation and harm being done to girls today. With Raising Girls he strives to spark a movement to end the trashing of girlhood; equipping parents to deal with the modern world, and getting the media off the backs of our daughters.

Raising Girls is powerful, practical and positive. Your heart, head and hands will be strengthened by its message.

Getting Real About Growing Up by Amrita Hobbs

This is a resource book for life. It speaks directly to the teenager and the young adult. It is also a resource for parents and anyone working with youth. It communicates hauntingly to the teenager in every adult. it is full of practical suggestions and things to do. Teen Speak, anecdotes and stories make Getting Real... about growing up! enriching and spiritually uplifting. Stories are a great way of communicating a point and make it easier to understand and empathise when written in such language. Teen Speak is an integral part of the book. It's great to hear the opinion of other young people. The style is diverse and effective. It inspires every reader to move beyond some of the limitations imposed on them from outside authority, their family background and the overcoming of childhood hurts. This book encourages readers to find their own uniqueness and express themselves in a powerful and effective way from a loving heart.

The Thundering Years: Rituals and Sacred Wisdom for Teens by Julie Tallard Johnson

Shows teens how to harness the intense emotions and drives of the late-teen years using wisdom from cultures around the world. Includes exercises, personal and community rituals, and resources that show how to successfully navigate the Thundering Years without heading toward violence, drug abuse, and other self-destructive behaviours. Inspiring quotations from many spiritual traditions as well as the words and real-life experiences of other young adults. Presents an honest view of the passions and pain that occur during this major life transition. According to native traditions, the Thundering Years are the time in life to listen to intense feelings, dreams, desires, and goals -- to be outrageous and even difficult. The Thundering Years are the teen years, the time when you are journeying into adulthood. They are exciting years, full of potential and creative energy, and they are painful years, full of turmoil and self-examination. Author Julie Tallard Johnson has collected wisdom from cultures around the world to help you survive your Thundering Years with your soul, creativity, and even sense of humour intact. She offers numerous techniques and traditions to help harness the powerful energy released during this time. She shows that when you connect with your thunder in a respectful way, you are given the confidence you need to accomplish all your dreams.

How to be a Woman by Caitlin Moran

Aimed at older girls/women but well worth reading- both serious and humorous at the same time! It's a good time to be a woman: we have the vote and the Pill, and we haven't been burnt as witches since 1727. However, a few nagging questions do remain...Why are we supposed to get Brazilians? Should we use Botox? Do men secretly hate us? And why does everyone ask you when you're going to have a baby? Part memoir, part rant, Caitlin answers the questions that every modern woman is asking.

I walk with beauty before me
I walk with beauty behind me
I walk with beauty above me
I walk with beauty below me
I walk with beauty all around me
As I walk the beauty way

I walk with beauty all around me
As I live my life the beauty way

May all my thoughts be beautiful
May all my words be beautiful
May all my actions be beautiful
As I live my life the beauty way

I walk with beauty all around me
As I live my life the beauty way

Chant by Navajo American Indians

Weaving woman
Intent, desire, longing
Manifestation
Visualisation
Picture perfect
Achieve, believe
Attract, react
Draw it in
From the web of life
Weaving woman
Make it so
See it, feel it
Third eye, heart connection
Spinning, scooping
Weaving in to being
Rachael 2004

Time of the month
Red Dark Sticky Tacky
Blood Bleeding Stench Swollen
Vulva Womb Pain Contracting
Tearing Flesh Ripping Inside
Deep Trickle Heavy Flow
Plug Stop Ignore No
Listen Calling Tired Slow
Rest Renew Cycle Begin again
Rachael 2003

A Period Limerick

There once was a woman from Gosham
Who took out her towels to chuck'em
But her husband said Heather
Your as light as a feather
But your towels are too heavy so
wash'em
NOTE: Always wash your sanitary
towels or you'll be stuck in an endless
bad poem like Heather!

By Tabitha aged 12

I honour you

I honour you
In circle gathered
In circle blessed
In circle joined
In circle one
She who weaves and writes and
dances and draws
Creative woman I honour you
She who look in the mirror of her
soul
Honest woman I honour you
She who looks fear in the face,
embraces it and laughs
Brave woman I honour you
She who stands at the gateway to
the worlds and holds the key for
those who would explore
Holy woman I honour you
She who soothes the salt tears with
the sweat of her brow
Compassionate woman I honour
you
She who sees the pot of gold in the
rainbows brilliant arc
Visionary woman I honour you
She whose hands labour to prepare
the fertile ground to plant, water,
weed and gather fruit

Abundant woman I honour you
She who listens and looks and
learns
Thinking woman I honour you
She who greets the dawn of the day
in all her beauty unclothed
Free woman I honour you
She who births and bleeds
Nurtures and knows
Loves and laughs
Dances and dreams
Sobs and smiles
Stumbles and stands
Gives and is grateful
And follows her path through life
with heart
Sister I honour you!

Helen Ramoutsaki

*Image: Woman dances in Menarche
celebration*

Moon Times
Organic Washable Pads, Panty Liners
Moon Sponges & Cups

www.moontimes.co.uk

Moon Times Washable Menstrual Products including:
Organic Cloth Pads & Panty Liners, Moon Sponges & Cups
and other products for the 'Green Minded' Woman!

"Whenever I have my period, I have the feeling that in spite of all the pain, discomfort and mess, I'm carrying around a sweet secret. So even though it's a nuisance, in a certain way I'm always looking forward to the time when I'll feel that secret inside me once again." **Anne Frank**

Reusable menstrual products are safer for your body and more cost effective; they are not a step back in time but a positive step towards our planet's well being! Moon Times offer alternatives to 'disposable' sanitary wear- products that last for years and save you £100's; being kind to your purse whilst being kind to the planet!
Moon Times Organic Pads and Panty Liners are the soft, comfortable alternative to disposables, free from bleaches, irritants and chemicals; made from breathable organic cotton, leaving you feeling confident and fresh!

Comments from customers:
'They look - and feel lovely - so soft!' *Becky*
'For the first time ever I'm really looking forward to bleeding!' *Tanya*
'They are so much more comfortable than ordinary pads! And prettier too. Thanks!'
Louise (age 14)
"I love using Moon Times ~ the best thing is never having to remember to buy more pads!" *Victoria*
'I use pads and a mooncup on heavy days.. I find both products fantastic!! Thanks for setting me free!!' *Mary*
'I was surprised at how comfortable they were, much better than disposable pads. They felt cosy and secure and felt like I was giving my "lady bits" a special treat with the fun patterns rather than the boring, medical style sanitary protection.' *Sarah*

Even if you only use cloth pads at night it will reduce the amount of sanitary waste we women produce with 'disposable' products.

In the UK alone, we buy more than 3 billion items of menstrual products every year, spending £349 million in 2010 on sanitary and 'feminine hygiene' products. What's more, disposable panty liners used between periods are increasing the size of the market, with sales of £56 million in 2010. Meanwhile, feminine hygiene wipes have seen the biggest growth, with sales of £4.8m in 2010. An average woman throws away an astonishing 125 to 150kg of tampons, pads and applicators in her lifetime.

Moon Times are an alternative to disposable sanitary products.

Cloth pads are an ideal gift for young women new to their menses and for new mothers who need soft cloth against their delicate tissue after giving birth. They can also be used by women who suffer from slight incontinence.

Moon Times are made with organic cotton flannelette and fair trade organic cotton. Inserts are available in organic cotton, hemp and towelling for extra absorbency. *Flannelette is both soft and absorbent* and used as the 'top' layer- next to your skin. You put an 'insert' (a small liner) inside the pocket of the pad (or a few if you are bleeding heavily) choosing cotton, hemp or towelling inserts. Pads have wings and fasten with press studs so they are very secure!

When you first use Moon Times products, it may seem as if your flow is heavier or even lighter than usual- this is natural- I believe that some of the chemicals used in other sanitary products can affect the amount we bleed-also we may not be used to seeing our blood that closely!

Moon Times are the only manufactures of hand made organic washable pads in the UK.
We also supply other 'moon time' products; moon cups & sponges, herbal teas, Women's Wisdom Booklets and much more. We support sustainable living and so use sustainable fabrics such as organic cotton and hemp.
Moon Times empower women in body appreciation, environmental awareness and self-respect through the use of eco menstrual products.
FFI or to buy on line go to
www.moontimes.co.uk
Use this code to get 10% off your order MENARCHE

Contributors:

Alexandra Pope lecturer on menstruation and menstrual health at naturopathic colleges, universities, community health centres and counselling organizations, she also holds one day workshops nationally and internationally on the wisdom of menstruation, cultivating female power and menstrual wellbeing, as well as speaking at conferences.

Anita Diamant Journalist and writer; author of the Red Tent

Dr Christiane Northrup a gynecologist who acknowledges the power of natural therapies and herbs, but also maintains that allopathic treatments, including surgery, are sometimes best. In Women's Bodies, Women's Wisdom she covers the treatment of many physical concerns--among them PMS, menstrual cramps, breast cancer, fibroids, endometriosis, infertility, depression, childbirth, abortion, cystitis, and menopause--explaining how many of these physical problems have roots in emotional upsets.

Dominique Sakoilsky Women's Health Advocate; active birth tutor, cranial sacral therapist , is the founder of the Healthy Cycles courses in Bristol, and Director at Relaxed Birth and Parenting.

Michelle Royce/ Spiraldancer author of- Moon Rites a feminine path to personal power, this book is designed to be used as a tool to enhance your self-knowledge, acceptance, and personal power.

Ro Ocean brave young woman sharing her experiences of her menarche!

And thanks to the women who shared their first period stories;
Suzanne Thomas
Debbie Bryer
Lucy Pearce
Brigit Strawbridge
and Anon!

About Rachael

Rachael Hertogs is a mother of 4 gorgeous children, 2 beautiful daughters; Tabitha 23 and Dorothy who is just 3, and 2 shining boys; Jericho just turned 21 and Emrys her womb blessing baby, 6 months old!

Rachael, her husband and 2 youngest live in the Wilds of West Wales where they run a small holding; growing veggies and playing with their chickens and ducks in the puddles and the sun!

She began her 'menstrual journey' when she started making cloth pads while Tabitha was a baby! This led her to explore her cyclical nature and find healthy ways to ease her PMT and work on her relationship to her body.

She became a massage therapist in her 20's, a Reiki Master in her 30's and trained as one of Miranda Grays Moon Mothers (giving Womb and Yoni Blessings and healings) and a doula in her 40's - along side working with addicts and single mums teaching relaxation techniques, massage and Reiki, running her Moon Times business, putting on menstrual health workshops, Mum and Daughter Days and running full moon womens groups and dark moon red tents!

She has had articles on celebrating our young women, natural contraception and positive menstruation published in Juno -natural parenting magazine.

She is a dedicated women's menstrual health advocate, business woman, workshop facilitator and member of The Red Web Foundation. Rachael is also the designer of the most environmentally friendly sanitary wear imaginable! Moon Times cloth Pads are made from organic cotton and hemp- and are pretty as well as kind to Mother Earth.

Her aim is to empower women in body appreciation, environmental awareness and self-respect through the use of eco menstrual products.

She believes a healthy appreciation of our bodies and ourselves as women can be learnt through menstruation and when women are aware of the benefits of a sustainable, healthy, economically viable and comfortable alternative, they appreciate the contribution they can make by choosing alternative menstrual products.

She also believes women deeply appreciate learning about alternative and positive ways to think about their bodies.

Her websites:

http://www.rachaelhertogs.co.uk

http://www.moontimes.co.uk

http://www.moontimes.co.uk/blog

http://www.jamsponge.co.uk/

Made in the USA
San Bernardino,
CA